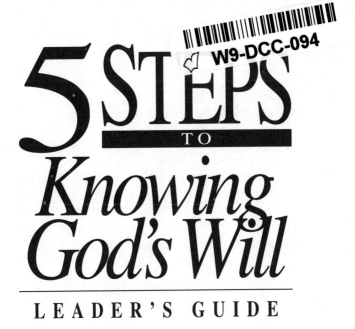

5 STEPS TO

Knowing God's Will

LEADER'S GUIDE

Bill Bright

NewLife
PUBLICATIONS
A MINISTRY OF CAMPUS CRUSADE FOR CHRIST

Five Steps to Knowing God's Will
Leader's Guide

Published by
New*Life* Publications
A ministry of Campus Crusade for Christ
P.O. Box 593684
Orlando, FL 32859-3684

Design and typesetting by Genesis Publications.

Printed in the United States of America.

Distributed in Canada by Campus Crusade for Christ of Canada, Surrey, B.C.

ISBN 1-56399-082-2

NewLife2000 is a registered service mark of Campus Crusade for Christ Inc.

Unless otherwise indicated, all Scripture references are taken from the *New International Version*, © 1973, 1978, 1984 by the International Bible Society. Published by Zondervan Bible Publishers, Grand Rapids, Michigan.

Scripture quotations designated TLB are from *The Living Bible*, © 1971 by Tyndale House Publishers, Wheaton, Illinois.

Scripture quotations designated NKJ are from the *New King James* version, © 1979, 1980, 1982 by Thomas Nelson Inc., Publishers, Nashville, Tennessee.

As a personal policy, Bill Bright has never accepted honorariums or royalties for his personal use. Any royalties from this book or the more than fifty books and booklets by Bill Bright are dedicated to the glory of God and designated to the various ministries of Campus Crusade for Christ/*NewLife2000*.

For more information, write:
Life Ministries—P.O. Box 40, Flemington Markets, N5W 2129, Australia
Campus Crusade for Christ of Canada—Box 300, Vancouver, B.C., V6C 2X3, Canada
Campus Crusade for Christ—Fairgate House, King's Road, Tyseley, Birmingham, B11 2AA, England
Campus Crusade for Christ—P.O. Box 8786, Auckland, New Zealand
Campus Crusade for Christ—Alexandra, P.O. Box 0205, Singapore, 9115, Singapore
Great Commission Movement of Nigeria—P.O. Box 500, Jos, Plateau State Nigeria, West Africa
Campus Crusade for Christ International—100 Sunport Lane, Orlando, FL 32809, USA

Contents

A Personal Word 5

How to Lead a Small Group Bible Study .9

Steps:

1 Desire to Know God's Will for Your Life 19

2 Avoid Misleading Formulas 37

3 Discover the Sound Mind Principle 59

4 Examine Your Options 75

5 By Faith, Follow God's Leading 95

A Personal Word

One summer morning, I received a call from Bailey Marks, Campus Crusade for Christ's International Vice President. He was concerned about the trip my wife, Vonette, and I were taking to the Philippines to meet with all of Campus Crusade's continental leaders. "Bill, security forces in Manila suspect a Communist threat against Campus Crusade during our upcoming meetings in Baguio City and the Lausanne conference in Manila," he informed me. "As president of our organization, you might be a special target."

"What's the situation there?" I asked.

"Communist terrorists are accelerating their campaign to overthrow the government. Because of our commitment to proclaim the gospel, Campus Crusade staff members may be in danger."

"What do the security forces want me to do?"

"Well, Bill, they strongly recommend a police escort to and from the conferences. And they want to station armed guards outside your hotel room at all times. Should I give them the go-ahead?"

I leaned forward in my chair and thought for a moment. Then I replied, "I'll discuss this with Vonette and call you back."

Later that night, I discussed Bailey's call with Vonette. We had to make a decision within a few hours and had several options to consider. We could cancel the meetings because of the risk to our staff and ourselves; we could agree to the recommended security measures; or we could proceed with our normal schedule and plans. Any of these choices could have detrimental outcomes, and could lead to our physical harm.

You probably have never encountered a situation like this, but I am sure you have faced decisions that would affect your life and the lives of others. Perhaps you wondered what God's will was under the circumstances. Or maybe you are facing a difficult personal decision and want to know what God would have you do.

We all struggle with questions about the future: How can I know God's plan for my life? Which job should I take? Is this the person God wants me to marry? Should I let my child participate in certain activities? Is this a good investment to make with my money? Which college should I attend? I am sure you could add many more to this list.

Most Christians are earnestly seeking direction for their lives, eager to know what God wants them to do. In fact, one of the questions I am asked most frequently is, "How can I know God's will for my life?" As I talk to believers around the world, I find that many are defeated, powerless, and fruitless because they do not understand how to find God's will for their lives.

Yet I am convinced that any obedient Christian can know God's will and experience a life of victory and joy. All it takes is understanding biblical principles for discerning God's will and applying them to our lives.

But perhaps you feel uncomfortable about letting God control your decisions. You may feel like the student who once asked me, "If I give my life to Christ, will I become a puppet?"

The answer is a resounding "No!" We never become puppets. We have the right of choice; we are free moral agents. God's Word assures us that He will guide and encourage us, but we must act as a result of our own wills. God does not force us to make certain choices.

Others feel that knowing God's will is a guessing game. They try to decide what God wants through "providential" circumstances, using an open-and-point method of searching the Bible, or any number of ways to try to read the mind of God.

We cannot claim God's promises and at the same time live by chance circumstances. He has given us guidelines in His

Word that will help us know what He has planned for us. He assures us that He has the perfect plan for our lives, one that will bring us joy, peace, and fruitfulness. These plans are not necessarily the easiest path to take nor the hardest, but they bring the greatest rewards.

In *Five Steps to Knowing God's Will*, we will discover a simple method of discerning God's will called the Sound Mind Principle. It has been formulated by applying scriptural principles and Spirit-controlled reason to everyday situations. Using the Sound Mind Principle will transform the way you approach difficult decisions, day-to-day choices, and even the way you view your future.

Vonette and I have been using the Sound Mind Principle for many decades. In fact, I applied that formula the day I talked with Bailey Marks. Right after his call, I weighed the seriousness of the threat and prayed for wisdom. Later that night, Vonette and I prayed, asking God to direct our decision. Then we talked about the pros and cons of the situation: our high visibility as leaders of a worldwide Christian movement; what God's purpose was for our trip; how our decision would affect others. We agreed that if someone planned to attack, there was not much the security forces could do. Yet we did not want to take unnecessary risks.

We knew that when the meetings in Baguio City ended, we would have to travel four hours by bus to Manila for the Lausanne Congress on Evangelism through what was believed to be terrorist territory. We also talked about the problems that accompany extra precautions. Not only would this cause delays for everyone involved, but the presence of guards would cause uneasiness for our staff and others.

After carefully weighing all the aspects of our options, we decided to ask for the least amount of security for our trip. We took comfort in knowing that our Lord would be with us every step of our journey. So I called Bailey and he made the arrangements. Later, I praised God that our trip to the Philippines went without incident.

Vonette and I try to live every day obeying God's will for our lives. God sometimes allows us to experience difficult trials, but once we know what God wants us to do, we proceed with confidence, leaving the results to Him.

Through the years, I have relied on a promise recorded in the book of James to help me discern God's will:

> If you want to know what God wants you to do, ask him, and he will gladly tell you, for he is always ready to give a bountiful supply of wisdom to all who ask him; he will not resent it. But when you ask him, be sure that you really expect him to tell you, for a doubtful mind will be as unsettled as a wave of the sea that is driven and tossed by the wind; and every decision you then make will be uncertain, as you turn first this way, and then that. If you don't ask with faith, don't expect the Lord to give you any solid answer (James 1:5–8, TLB).

From these verses, I have discovered two very important truths: ask for wisdom and ask in faith. This is the foundation for all of my choices.

Like me, you probably have found that God's holy Word does not give specific instructions for each situation we encounter. In fact, some people have suggested that the Bible is so outdated that it cannot give us the answers to our modern-day problems. That is not true. Using the principles God has given us in His Word, we can find our way through the maze of choices and decisions we must make every day of our lives.

If you are struggling with how to know God's will for your life, take heart. These lessons will help you discern His will for your daily and life decisions. By the time you finish studying these five Steps, you will be ready to examine the choices you must make and discern God's will for each of them. In addition, knowing our heavenly Father better and seeking Him more fully will make you more like our wonderful Savior and Lord, Jesus Christ. My prayer is that through this Bible study, you will get excited about stepping out in faith, confident that you are in God's will.

How to Lead a Small Group Bible Study

Perhaps you feel less than confident about leading a small group Bible study. If God has led you to be a leader, He will give you the power and wisdom to accomplish the task. You do not need to be a theologian, Bible scholar, or great teacher to guide a group in studying this material. God uses ordinary people who have a heart for Him and who make themselves available to do His will.

Personal preparation is a vital first step to becoming a godly leader. To be an effective leader:

- You should have previously, by faith, received Jesus Christ as your Savior and Lord.[1]

- You should know the reality of living moment by moment in the power of the Holy Spirit.[1]

- You should have a heart for God and for His truths as revealed in His holy Word, the Bible.

- You should desire to help others learn these truths and be willing to devote time and effort to leading a group.

If you meet these simple requirements, you are ready to assemble your group. I would encourage you to also have a growing awareness of the power of prayer and the spiritual and physical benefits of fasting for personal revival.[2]

---

[1] I encourage you to read these booklets: the *Four Spiritual Laws* and *Have You Made the Wonderful Discovery of the Spirit-Filled Life?* Order from your favorite bookseller or from New*Life* Publications at (800) 235-7255.

[2] See my book *The Coming Revival* for more information about fasting with prayer (available from your favorite bookseller or New*Life* Publications).

Assembling Your Study Group

The first and most important step is to pray for God's leading and blessing. Then invite your friends to attend or announce plans for your Bible study to others in your workplace, dormitory, or neighborhood. Often those who have received Christ as Savior as a result of your witness will be interested in participating. New Christians and others who need spiritual follow-up are likely prospects for your group as well. Believers who are going through difficult circumstances will benefit from this Bible study. Choose the people you think would be most interested, pray about their involvement, then visit each one personally.

Keep your group small to avoid losing a feeling of intimacy. With eight to twelve people, group members will feel freer to interact and to discuss the lesson material and any difficult choices they may be facing. You will also have more time to give your students individual attention as they begin to apply biblical truths in their lives.

Avoid pressuring anyone to join your group. At the same time, do not have a negative or apologetic attitude. The best way to promote interest and enthusiasm is to be interested and enthusiastic yourself. As you pray and wait on God, He will lead you to those He has chosen for your study.

Once you have identified interested participants, select a meeting place and time for your Bible study that is convenient for those who will attend. If several days lapse between your initial contact and the first study session, remind group members with a note or phone call.

Be sure to order a Study Guide (available from your favorite Christian bookseller or New*Life* Publications) for each member of your group.

Guidelines for Leading

The Leader's Guide is carefully designed to help you guide your students' discovery of spiritual principles and to show how these truths can be applied to their lives. Your main activity will be studying the Scriptures, and any discussion should follow the study outline in the lesson plan.

The following guidelines will help you lead the sessions:

- Bring extra Bibles and pencils for students to use during the study time.

- Create an informal atmosphere so you and your group can get acquainted. Address each person by name, and introduce new members before the discussion begins.

- Keep your Bible open at all times. The lesson material uses the *New International Version*.

- Be yourself. Depend on the Holy Spirit to work through the person you are, not through an artificial "spiritual leader" image that you would like to project.

- Don't be bound to your notes. Maintain eye contact with your group.

- Center the discussion around your students. A group leader is a discussion guide, not a lecturer. You should be prepared to suggest ideas, give background material, and ask questions to keep the conversation lively and relevant, but do not dominate the discussion. Instead, draw out comments from your students. The informal nature of a small group study is ideal for helping students learn from each other as well as from the things you say. (See the following section on how to encourage participation.)

- If a student is saying something pertinent, refrain from inserting your own thoughts. When he finishes, clarify and summarize if necessary.

- Avoid controversial theological teachings that could cause confusion among group members.

- Get involved in the lives of your group members. Plan extra time for informal fellowship with individual members or the entire group. Communicating the basic truths of the Christian life is more than passing on information; it is sharing life experiences. Help members put into practice the truths you are teaching. The way you model and mentor through your personal example will have a far greater impact on your group than any of the words you say in a meeting.

- Be punctual about beginning and closing the session.

Keep in mind that each group has its own personality—some groups are active, others more subdued. Adapt your leadership style to fit your group. Remember, your most important quality as a leader is to be open to the Holy Spirit's guidance as you help your students explore and apply the lessons they are learning.

How to Encourage Participation

Since your Bible study group will consist of Christians at different levels of spiritual maturity, a few may already be familiar with some of the content while for others it will be completely new. Your objective in this Bible study is to help develop the spiritual maturity of all your group members and train them to follow God's will in each decision.

Here are some suggestions for encouraging members to participate and for making the discussion time interesting and practical:

- To create a casual, intimate setting, arrange chairs in a circle or sit around a table if you have a small group.

- After reading the Bible passage, invite a member to summarize the passage in his own words before asking any questions about it.

- During the discussion time, avoid embarrassing anyone. When you ask a question of a member, be sure he answers it aptly. If he stumbles, help him along and make him feel that he did answer the question, at least in part. Compliment him on his response.

- When you ask a question, allow time for students to think before continuing. Then listen to their answers rather than mentally planning what you will say next. Remember that you are teaching people, not lessons.

- If you sense confusion about a question you ask, restate it in different words or from another point of view. Define all unusual words.

- Keep the discussion relevant and personal. To redirect the discussion, restate the question or ask for the answers to the next question. If a person asks a question that is off the topic, tactfully explain that it would be best not to take class time to discuss it. Offer to help answer the question after the study session is over.

- Stimulate conversation by asking questions such as: "What do you think this passage means?" "What can we learn from this passage about God, Christ, ourselves, our responsibilities, our relationships with others?"

- To help students apply the passage personally, ask, "What significance does this have for us today?" "What does this mean to you?" "How does (or will) it affect your life?"

- Often a great deal can be learned by disagreeing over a passage. To keep the discussion from turning into an argument, however, remind everyone that you are studying what the Bible says about a subject. The Bible is your final authority.

- Keep the discussion moving. If you cover the material too quickly, the study will be shallow; if you go too slowly, it will be tedious and boring. The lessons may include more material than you need, so do not spend too much time on any one section, but be sure you cover each major point.

- At the end of the discussion, ask someone to summarize the points that have been made. Be sure to guide the final summary and application.

- Make the group time enjoyable. Allow extra time after each session for social interaction, refreshments, and individual counseling.

Objectives of the Five-Week Study

During this study, your objectives are to help your students do the following:

1. **Understand God's attributes and how they apply to His trustworthiness.** For some Christians, misconceptions about who God is and how He relates to us create a barrier to obeying His will. This material will help students realize how loving and faithful God is and how we can trust Him to lead us into what is best for our lives.

2. **Recognize misleading formulas to discerning God's will.** Many people rely on chance or other unscriptural methods to decide what God's will is for their lives. This study will help students examine these methods to see if they really follow biblical principles.

3. **Commit to following God's will.** Sometimes the main barrier to obeying God's will is unwillingness to follow His commands. Through this study your group members will be challenged to examine their commitment to God's will.

4. **Begin practicing the Sound Mind Principle.** This principle will give your students practical steps to take in discerning God's will. Encourage them to apply God's Word and common sense to any decision they make.

How to Use the Lesson Plans

To teach this series of lessons effectively, study each part of the lesson before the group meeting. *There is no substitute for preparation.* Studying the lesson thoroughly will enable you to lead the discussion with confidence. If you take shortcuts in your preparation time, your group will not learn the principles effectively.

Prepare for each session by doing the following:

- Pray for the individuals in the group. Keep a list of each person's special needs and refer to it during your personal prayer time.

- Thank God for what He will teach all of you.
- Reread the objectives of the study.
- Review the session outline.
- Study the verses and answers to the questions in each lesson. Since the answers are printed in your Leader's Guide, you may be tempted to skip this step. However, familiarity with the Scripture passages and answers will help you during the group discussion.

Each lesson includes the following main parts:

Focus

This is a summary of the topic covered in the lesson.

Objectives

These are the main goals of the lesson. To help your students meet them and to keep the lesson on track, remember these objectives as you prepare and as you guide the discussion. A helpful technique is to jot the goals in your Leader's Guide where you want to emphasize them.

Session Scriptures

These verses will give you an overview of the material covered in the lesson. You may want to read these verses in your quiet time during the week.

Outline

The outline presents the structure of the Bible study. Use it as a map to help you see where the lesson is heading.

Leader's Preparation

This material is for your enrichment and instruction in presenting the lesson and tells you what to bring to the session. Review this section just before you come to class.

The Bible Study Session

To help you as you guide the lesson, the leader's directions are in bold type, and the answers to questions are in parentheses and italicized.

Sharing

This opening time is designed to help your group share their progress in applying the previous lesson. Relate personal joys and concerns as well as experiences that you or other members of your group have had. Set a friendly, non-threatening tone for the discussion time. Before beginning the lesson, open with prayer, asking the Holy Spirit to guide the study and prepare your hearts for God's Word.

Discussion Starter

Your opening question and the resulting discussion should stimulate thinking, but not necessarily supply answers. Guide the discussion by interjecting further questions. Do not correct wrong answers at this time, but use the discussion to make your students think.

Lesson Development

This section gives directions for leading the Bible study. The ideas will enable you to help group members understand each principle studied. Adapt the teaching suggestions to your group size and personalities and to your leadership style. When reading Scripture passages, use a variety of methods. For example:

- Read the passage aloud while the group follows along.

- Have everyone read it silently.

- Ask a different person to read each verse or passage. (This is preferred.)

- Ask one member to read while the others follow along.

Application

This section will help you challenge your group members to apply what they have learned. Many of the application points should be considered by each member privately. Your role is to guide their thinking and lead them to personal decisions.

Closing and Prayer

This is a good time to ask for any additional comments or questions on the lesson material. Then encourage one of the members to lead the group in prayer. Also use this time to pray for specific needs and concerns expressed by the students.

Follow-Up

This section contains suggestions for helping your group members outside the lesson time and for planning fellowship gatherings. Adapt them for your group's particular situation.

Student Lesson Plan

Located at the end of each lesson, this plan is a duplicate of the Study Guide. Instructions in the Leader's Guide tell when to use the Study Guide material. Encourage members to record their answers in their Study Guides during the group time and refer to them between sessions.

I pray that, during your study, God will open your mind and heart to the truths presented here. As you help others discover the dynamics of spiritual growth, you will see changed lives. While your group may be small, the impact of what you do will multiply in the years ahead as you and your group members follow God's leading into greater ministry and fruitful living.

STEP 1

Desire to Know God's Will for Your Life

Focus

Understanding God's character will help us to love Him, obey Him, and trust Him to guide our decisions. Praising Him will help us keep our focus on Him.

Objectives

This session will help students to:

- *Realize* that God's will is the best for us
- *Understand* the attributes of God
- *Discuss* the part each attribute plays in our decision to trust God
- *Develop* a lifestyle of praise and thanksgiving

Session Scriptures

Jeremiah 9:23,24; 29:11; John 10:10; 15:5,8,11; Romans 1:17; 8:28; 12:2; Colossians 1:9,10; Hebrews 11:6

Outline

   I. Discovering the importance of God's will
  II. Getting to know our heavenly Father
 III. Exploring God's attributes
 IV. Developing a lifestyle of continuous praise

Leader's Preparation

As God's children, we receive many wonderful things from our loving Father. He wants what is best for us and wants us to seek His will so we can enjoy the fullness of knowing Him (John 10:10). For us to fully experience God's perfect will in our lives, He asks us to yield completely to Him. At any time He may ask us to surrender our own plans, but we can be assured that what He offers is much better.

Many Christians, however, do not really comprehend the importance of knowing and following God's will. In addition, each participant in your group will come with a different attitude toward God's plan for his life. Some may have a deep desire to know God's will but not understand how to find it. Others may struggle with trusting God with their decisions. Still others may find it hard to stick with God's plan for their lives once a choice has been made. You may have some members who make impulsive decisions, then expect God to bless them. And a few may be skilled at listening to God's voice and following through with His plans.

As the leader, be sensitive to the needs and attitudes of your group members. Respect their choices, even if they do not seem logical to you, because God may be leading them in a direction that is not clear to you. However, if group members make decisions that are contrary to God's Word, gently lead them to the appropriate Scripture passages. In some cases, you may wish to counsel an individual privately.

Since some issues shared during the sessions may be sensitive topics, before each session ask group members to keep confidential all personal information brought out during the discussion. Do not force anyone to reveal issues they wish to keep private. If you feel information that a member is beginning to share is too personal, suggest that you and the member discuss it and pray together after the session.

Also keep in mind that no decision is too trivial to bring before our loving God. It is important to answer all questions about knowing God's will for our daily choices. Because these five Steps are part of a process, review the Focus statements and Objectives of all five lessons before beginning the study. This will give you an overview of the Sound Mind Principle.

This Bible study series begins by focusing on God. To help your group members develop greater confidence in trusting God with decisions, in this session you will study several of God's characteristics. The group will also learn that praising God will help them remain focused on Him during difficult times. This lesson will help your members deepen their relationship with God and have the right attitude in applying the remaining Steps.

The following material on the attributes of God is for your personal study. Look up references for each attribute during your quiet time, then praise God for that characteristic. If your Bible lists cross-references that give similar information, study those verses to discover more about the attribute.

God is self-sufficient, independent of any need. He is the source of everything and (unlike us) needs nothing. Psalm 50:12; Acts 17:24,25

God is immutable, or not subject to change. His nature is constant throughout eternity. He cannot get worse or better because He is perfect. Malachi 3:6; Hebrews 1:12; James 1:17

God is one. Though existing in three persons, He is one God with one essence. He is one in quantity, so He has unity. He is one in quality, so He has simplicity. He is one in wholeness, with His entire being set apart from everything else. Deuteronomy 6:4; Matthew 28:19

God is intellect. He is knowledge and understanding, therefore, He knows all things. He is wisdom, so He is able to apply His knowledge to attain the best result. He is all truth and incapable of lying. Numbers 23:19; Psalm 147:5; Romans 11:33

God is good. He is morally pure and excellent. Everything He does shows His goodness and His purity. Psalm 143:10; Mark 10:18

For the first meeting, bring a *Five Steps to Knowing God's Will* Study Guide for each person attending, extra Bibles, pencils, 3×5 cards, and a large sheet of paper or flip chart.

The Bible Study Session

Sharing (5 minutes)

Greet members warmly as they arrive, and allow them a few minutes to get acquainted with each other. Give each person a Study Guide and a 3×5 card. Ask them to write down their name, address, and telephone number, then collect the cards.

Ask students to open their Study Guides to the Contents page and read through the titles of the five Steps. Briefly describe each of the lessons by giving the Focus statements. Thank each person for coming and express your excitement about the new Bible study.

Discussion Starter (5 minutes)

Read the following vignette:

Kim and Leonard put themselves on a tight budget. They had used credit until their finances were in a shambles. When the Lord convicted them about their debt, they began paying off their credit cards and small loans.

One morning, Kim's mother called to say that she was coming for a two-week visit. Kim was excited. Her mother was not a believer, and Kim felt this was a good opportunity to talk to her mother about a relationship with Jesus Christ.

One problem remained: Kim and Leonard lived in a one-bedroom apartment. Where would Kim's mother sleep?

Leonard noticed a sale ad in the newspaper for sofa sleepers. That afternoon, he and Kim went to the furniture store to check out the sale. Kim found a sofa that would fit nicely in their living room and the colors were perfect!

The salesman explained that the store would not charge interest for six months and that the payments were low.

After spending a few moments discussing what to do, Kim and Leonard decided that the situation had worked together so well that buying the sofa must be God's will.

Discuss:

- Do you think Kim and Leonard made the right choice? Why?

- How would you have approached the same situation?

- What part does common sense play in discerning God's will?

Lesson Development (35–45 minutes)

Discovering the Importance of God's Will

Begin by saying: All sincere Christians wrestle with the question of what God's will is for their lives. Whether it is the choice of a career or mate, the use of time or money, or any other option, we need to understand biblical principles about making decisions according to God's will and not our own.

Christians who seek and obey God's guidance in making their decisions will experience a supernatural life of meaning and fulfillment. Such a life can be lived by any Christian if only he understands and applies certain simple biblical principles. During this Bible study, we will be learning about the steps to applying God's will to any decision we might face.

Ask:

- Why should we be concerned about God's will? *(He is our heavenly Father who loves us as His dear children; He understands us better than we understand ourselves; God's will is the best plan for our lives.)*

- What might happen if we do not follow His will? *(We will make wrong choices; we will not achieve the best in our lives; we will fall into sin.)*

Say: Jesus promises us an abundant life. **Read John 10:10.** But many Christians deprive themselves of this full, abundant life by failing to obey God's will. Because they do not comprehend the true character and nature of God—His abso-

lute love, grace, wisdom, power, sovereignty, and holiness—
they foolishly choose to live according to their own plans rather
than the will of God. Others have such a distorted view of God
that they think of Him as a tyrant to appease. Being afraid of
God, they cannot trust Him with their decisions. Other sincere
Christians want to do the will of God, but do not know how to
discover it for themselves. Many just give up and do what
comes easy. Let's look at four reasons why it is so important to
know and obey God's will for our lives.

**With each of the following points, read the verses and
discuss how the point relates to the importance of God's
will to our lives. The points are given in the Study Guide.
Encourage students to take notes during the discussion.**

1. God's will is the best for us—Romans 12:2 *(We need never
   fear accepting the will of God. His will is described as good,
   pleasing, and perfect.)*

2. God's will reflects His deep love for us—Jeremiah 29:11;
   Romans 8:28. *(God promises to work on our behalf because
   He loves us so much. When we follow His leading, we put
   ourselves in the center of His care and protection.)*

3. God desires that we know and experience His will for our
   lives—Colossians 1:9,10. *(Because God wants us to benefit
   from following His superior plan, He will reveal His will for
   us. He will guide us just as He did the Old and New Testament believers.)*

4. God's will results in a life of fruitfulness, joy, and blessing
   while bringing glory to God—John 15:5,8,11. *(Our choice
   is to follow God's will and experience joy and accomplish
   much for His kingdom, or to follow our own inclinations
   and experience sorrow, heartache, and pain, and accomplish nothing of eternal value.)*

Read: In order to trust God for the big things, we have to
have a big God. And our God is a God who can do anything.

Astronomers inform us that there are more than 100 billion
galaxies. Our Milky Way galaxy is little more than a grain of

sand in all of creation. It logically follows that our little Earth is like a grain of sand in our galaxy. Man is at least a microbe on the "grain of sand" we call Earth. It is this vast universe that biblical writers in Hebrews 1, Colossians 1, and John 1 tell us was created by God the Son. He holds everything together by the Word of His command, yet He lovingly watches over man. When we see God from this perspective, we have no trouble loving Him, trusting Him, and obeying Him.

   Therefore, the first and foremost step in following God's will is to trust Him with our decisions; we must believe that God's will is the best possible plan for our lives. <u>Just as in any intimate relationship, to trust God we must first know Him</u>.

Ask:

- How do relationships with other people develop into close friendships? *(By spending time with a person; by getting to know that person as an individual.)*

- How does knowing a person well help you to trust that person? Specifically, what characteristics help you trust someone in particular situations? *(When you know that a person is honest, you can trust him with financial areas; when you know that a person is caring, you can trust him with your feelings; when you know that a person is reliable, you can trust him with long-range plans.)*

- How does this concept apply to knowing God? *(We need to get to know what God is like so we can trust Him in all areas of our lives.)*

Say: The person who has a realistic view of God will have no trouble saying, "Lord, I trust you with every detail in every area of my life. I will go where You want me to go and do what You want me to do."

Getting to Know Our Heavenly Father

Before we can discern God's will, we need to know Him intimately. This illustration shows how important it is to know God as our loving heavenly Father.

Read: A young woman picked up a book to read, but found it dull and boring. She soon laid it down. Shortly afterward, she met a young man with whom she fell in love. During their engagement, she learned that he was the author of the book she had found so boring. She began to read the book again. This time, she read it from cover to cover with great enthusiasm.

Why did she have a renewed interest? Because now she knew and loved the author. In a similar way, when we come to know and love our heavenly Father, His book—the Bible—becomes alive and vital to us.

As we have discussed, all relationships develop by spending time with the other person. This is also true of our relationship with God. He, of course, is perfect and His qualities are all perfect, too. Knowing more about Him and spending time with Him gives us more confidence to trust Him.

Explain what an attribute is: An expensive jewel has various aspects, called *facets*, each showing a different side of the gem's nature. Our human natures also have many facets, which are revealed by circumstances and trials that occur in our lives. God is that way as well. We see the many facets of His nature as He interacts with His creation. These facets we call attributes.

An attribute is a distinguishing characteristic, something that identifies or describes someone. God's attributes distinguish Him from everyone else and are an expression of His nature.

Ask students to turn to their neighbor and together identify four or five attributes of God that they already know. Write these qualities on a large piece of paper or flip chart. Discuss how each makes God unique.

Exploring God's Attributes

Explain: Exploring the attributes of God is like exploring space—He is beyond our human ability to comprehend. Although God is knowable, He is incomprehensible. Although He can live in us, He transcends all of creation. If He did not reveal Himself to us, we could never know what He is like. Since He does reveal Himself, we can understand in part who He is.

Let us look at a few key attributes of God and their significance to us. **NOTE: This lesson includes more material on God's attributes than you can cover. Study the attributes that seem most appropriate for your group. Be sure to leave enough time to adequately cover the next section.**

Say: Read each verse that accompanies the attributes under the heading "Exploring God's Attributes" in your Study Guide, then answer the questions. You may study the attributes we do not cover in your quiet time with God.

Give students several minutes to complete the questions, then read the following definition of praise:

> Praise is the expression of our devotion to God. It is the channel by which we communicate our honor and respect for Him. A lifestyle of praise and thanksgiving to God cleanses us from self-centeredness and enables us to focus on Him.

Say: As we learn about each of God's attributes, let us praise and thank Him for that characteristic.

For each of the following attributes, discuss the questions as a group, then ask this question: What changes should take place in your life now that you know that this attribute is true of God? **Allow for responses, then have students praise God for that particular attribute, using one-sentence prayers as they feel led to do so. Encourage students to focus on God while they pray. Emphasize that God does not care as much about the words we speak when we pray as He does the attitude of our heart. Conclude with a one-sentence praise of your own.**

God Is Love—1 John 4:8

> What it means: *(Since God's very nature is love, everything He does is characterized by love. His love is endless and unconditional.)*

> What it means in my life: *(God loves me. He always has and He always will, no matter what I do. Nothing can separate me from His love.)*

God Is Sovereign—2 Samuel 7:22; Isaiah 40:25

> What it means: *(Nothing or no one can compare with God. He is above all and rules everything.)*

> What it means in my life: *(God deserves honor because He is far above us as finite and limited humans. He must be the only God in my life.)*

God Is Holy—Isaiah 6:3; 1 Peter 1:15,16

Lamb of God

> What it means: *(God is totally separate from evil and sin. His nature is completely <u>pure and spotless</u>. The Old Testament repeatedly emphasizes God's holiness, such as His distance from the people on Mount Sinai, the division of the holy of holies in the tabernacle and temple, and the laws He set for His people.)*

> What it means in my life: *(I can approach God only through the blood of Jesus Christ. God will never ask me to do anything that is wrong or against His principles.)*

God Is Faithful—1 Corinthians 1:9; 1 Thessalonians 5:24

> What it means: *(God is dependable. He keeps the promises in His Word. He is always working on my behalf.)*

> What it means in my life: *(I can believe the Bible. I can always depend on God to do what He says He will do. Regardless of how bad my circumstances appear, knowing God is faithful gives me hope.)*

God Is Righteous and Just—Psalm 89:14; 145:17; 2 Thessalonians 1:6,7

> What it means: *(He is completely right and fair in all moral dealings. He cannot sin and will not break His own just, moral laws. His Word is always true and upright.)*

> What it means in my life: *(God will be completely fair and right with me, so I can continue to trust Him even when I experience injustice or unfairness here on earth. When I think others do not get what they deserve, I can trust God to reward or punish them in a way that is perfectly fair.)*

God Knows Everything—Psalm 139:1–4; Hebrews 4:13; 1 John 3:20

What it means: *(God knows all of our thoughts and plans. Even before time began, He knew exactly what would happen throughout all time.)*

What it means in my life: *(God knows and understands me completely. He knows, better than I do, what is best for me. I cannot hide anything from God, nor can anyone else. I can have confidence that He knows the answers to my problems and the direction of my life.)*

God Is Spirit—John 4:24

What it means: *(This refers to God's invisible nature. Since by nature God is Spirit, He is not limited in any physical way by space or time.)*

What it means in my life: *(He lives through me by dwelling in me and giving me His power. Because He is not limited by flesh, God is much greater than I can ever imagine.)*

God Is Eternal—Psalm 90:2

What it means: *(God is outside time. He had no beginning; He will have no end.)*

What it means in my life: *(God will always be there. His perspective is greater than mine.)*

God Is Everywhere—Jeremiah 23:24; Psalm 139:7,8

What it means: *(Unlimited by space, God can be everywhere at once. There is no place in the universe to which we can go that will separate us from Him.)*

What it means in my life: *(No one can hide from God. No matter where I go, I can be assured that He is with me.)*

God Is All Powerful—Job 42:2; Jeremiah 32:17; Matthew 19:26

What it means: *(God can do anything that is in harmony with His perfect nature. God's power is the source of hope and comfort for those who believe in Him. He is the provider and sustainer of all things.)*

What it means in my life: *(Any problem I have can be handled by God who has all power.)*

Say: There is much, much more to God than the few attributes we've covered. Understanding that God is eternal and that He is not limited as we are gives us great confidence in His ability to know our needs, understand our heart's desires, and lead us in the correct path. God has revealed His divine attributes through His Word and through the person of Jesus Christ. We are made in His image, and He desires that we know Him and trust Him. **Read Jeremiah 9:23,24.**

Developing a Lifestyle of Continuous Praise

Say: One way we can focus on God's perfect characteristics and deepen our trust in His plan for our life is by praising and thanking Him. The Bible assures us that God inhabits the praise of His people (Psalm 22:3). We are also commanded to give thanks in all things (1 Thessalonians 5:18). Let us take time to look into our Lord's eyes with the wonder and excitement of a child and express our love for Him. Another way we can praise God is by telling others how much we appreciate and adore Him.

Developing a lifestyle of continuous praise and thanksgiving is no easy task. Not only will we face Satan's resistance, but our own feelings may become an obstacle. Feelings change and will fail us during times of stress. Have you ever tried to thank God when your children came down with the chicken pox or your husband lost his job? Do you find praise easy when your wife continually leaves the bathroom cluttered or your teenager wrecks the car? How do you feel when you are broke and your taxes are due, or your college roommate is grumpy and unloving?

Making praise a part of our lifestyle takes an act of the will. We cannot rely on feelings; we must consciously adopt a pattern of appreciation. Simply put, we can either decide to be bitter, critical, and depressed, or we can choose to praise and thank God.

You may say, "This sounds terribly simplistic. I live in a world where this is impossible to do." Let me assure you, it takes practice to reach a consistent pattern of praise.

Ask the following two questions, allow for discussion, then summarize with the italicized points. Encourage students to write their conclusions in their Study Guides.

- In what ways can praise open channels of communication and build unity between us and God? *(Obstructions like fear, pride, busyness, and doubt all clog the channels of communication. Praise dissolves these blockages by focusing our attention on God. Praise also prepares our hearts for a deeper, more intimate relationship with God.)*

- How do praise and thanksgiving affect our emotions? *(Genuine praise lifts our spirits. Praising God energizes our faith, directs our prayers, takes our minds off our problems, and focuses our thoughts on God's power rather than our weakness. Thanksgiving transforms our negative dispositions into positive attitudes.)*

Say: Here are four practical steps you can take to make praise a way of life. These steps are listed in your Study Guides. **Read the points and discuss how each may be applied to your daily routine. Ask students to jot their thoughts in their Study Guides.**

1. *Look for God's presence in every area of your life.* Search out ways God is working in your life that you may not have noticed before. Praise God for the characteristics that made His work in your life possible. Keep these ways fresh in your mind, especially when you are tempted to focus on negative thoughts.

2. *Show your gratitude regularly.* Too often we take for granted our most precious friend, Jesus Christ. Look for the blessings He has given you and the things He has done for you, and thank Him for them.

3. *Offer a sacrifice of praise.* Sometimes praising God in the midst of a difficult circumstance calls for sacrifice—it may cost us our pride and self-will. The apostle Paul admonishes, "By Him [Jesus Christ] let us continually offer the sacrifice of praise to God, that is, the fruit of our lips, giving thanks to His name" (Hebrews 13:15, NKJ).

According to the Scriptures, God required Israel to bring their best offering to His altar for sacrifice. The offering had to cost each Israelite his best bull or lamb (Leviticus 22:21). This principle holds true in praise as well. Unless our offering costs us something, it is not a sacrifice (2 Samuel 24:24). Praise that springs sacrificially from our innermost being, despite our circumstances, pleases God.

4. *Share the attributes of God with others.* Publicly praise God for His specific characteristics and how he displays them in your life. Develop a habit of giving God credit for what He does in your life. This may mean telling people that God was with you in an everyday situation or explaining how God helped you determine the direction in your life. As you give Him credit, you will focus on what God is doing in your life rather than on what others may think you are doing to help yourself.

Application (5 minutes)

Go over the Action Point in the Student Lesson Plan, encouraging the students to use praise in their quiet time with God during the week.

Closing and Prayer (5 minutes)

Record individual prayer needs or praises on each member's 3×5 card. Encourage students to pray for each other between sessions. Close by praying aloud for each person by name and ask God to give your group a closeness and a desire to serve Him through this Bible study.

Follow-Up

To build relationships among members, plan an outside activity for your group, such as going out for an ice cream sundae, having a meal together, or attending a sports event. Refer to the group's prayer requests during your quiet time with God as you pray for your students.

Student Lesson Plan

Discovering the Importance of God's Will

1. *God's will is the best for us*—Romans 12:2.

2. *God's will reflects His deep love for us*—Jeremiah 29:11; Romans 8:28.

3. *God desires that we know and experience His will for our lives*—Colossians 1:9,10.

4. *God's will results in a life of fruitfulness, joy, and blessing while bringing glory to God*—John 15:5,8,11.

Exploring God's Attributes

God Is Love—1 John 4:8

What it means:

What it means in my life:

God Is Sovereign—2 Samuel 7:22; Isaiah 40:25

What it means:

What it means in my life:

God Is Holy—Isaiah 6:3; 1 Peter 1:15,16

What it means:

What it means in my life:

God Is Faithful—1 Corinthians 1:9; 1 Thessalonians 5:24

What it means:

What it means in my life:

God Is Righteous and Just—Psalm 89:14; 145:17; 2 Thessalonians 1:6,7

What it means:

What it means in my life:

God Knows Everything—Psalm 139:1–4; Hebrews 4:13; 1 John 3:20

What it means:

What it means in my life:

God Is Spirit—John 4:24

What it means:

What it means in my life:

God Is Eternal—Psalm 90:2

What it means:

What it means in my life:

God Is Everywhere—Jeremiah 23:24; Psalm 139:7,8

What it means:

What it means in my life:

God Is All Powerful—Job 42:2; Jeremiah 32:17; Matthew 19:26

What it means:

What it means in my life:

Definition of praise: Praise is the expression of our devotion to God. It is the channel by which we communicate our honor and respect for Him. A lifestyle of praise and thanksgiving to God cleanses us from self-centeredness and enables us to focus on Him.

Developing a Lifestyle of Continuous Praise

- In what ways can praise open channels of communication and build unity between us and God?
- How do praise and thanksgiving affect our emotions?

Here are four practical steps you can take to make praise a way of life.

1. *Look for God's presence in every area of your life.* Search out ways God is working in your life that you may not have noticed before. Praise God for the characteristics that made His work in your life possible. Keep these ways fresh in your mind, especially when you are tempted to focus on negative thoughts.

2. *Show your gratitude regularly.* Too often we take for granted our most precious friend, Jesus Christ. Look for the blessings He has given you and the things He has done for you, and thank Him for them.

3. *Offer a sacrifice of praise.* Sometimes praising God in the midst of a difficult circumstance calls for sacrifice—it may cost us our pride and self-will. The apostle Paul admonishes, "By Him [Jesus Christ] let us continually offer the sacrifice of praise to God, that is, the fruit of our lips, giving thanks to His name" (Hebrews 13:15, NKJ).

   According to the Scriptures, God required Israel to bring their best offering to His altar for sacrifice. The offering had to cost each Israelite his best bull or lamb (Leviticus 22:21). This principle holds true in praise as well. Unless our offering costs us something, it is not a sacrifice (2 Samuel 24:24). Praise that springs sacrificially from our innermost being, despite our circumstances, pleases God.

4. *Share the attributes of God with others.* Publicly praise God for His specific characteristics and how he displays them in your life. Develop a habit of giving God credit for what He does in your life. This may mean telling people that God was with you in an everyday situation or explaining how God helped you determine the direction in your life. As you give Him credit, you will focus on what God is doing in your life rather than on what others may think you are doing to help yourself.

Action Point: Below are Bible verses that reveal some of the attributes of God. This week, look up the verses and praise God for each attribute during your quiet time.

Day 1   Psalm 25:5
           Psalm 50:6

Day 2   Psalm 66:3
           Psalm 77:13
           Psalm 111:3

Day 3   Psalm 121:2
           Isaiah 44:6
           Joel 2:13

Day 4   Micah 7:18
           Mark 10:18

Day 5   Luke 1:37
           John 3:33
           Acts 10:34

Day 6   1 Corinthians 1:25
           1 Corinthians 14:33

Day 7   Hebrews 6:18
           James 1:13
           1 John 1:5

STEP

2

Avoid Misleading Formulas

Focus

Using misleading formulas in our desire to discern and obey God's will can lead to disastrous results. Examining the way we make decisions can help us see how we arrive at these choices.

Objectives

This session will help students to:

- *Discover* the sources that can influence their decisions
- *Recognize* misleading formulas for making decisions
- *Understand* the results of relying on these formulas
- *Examine* past decisions to discover the formulas underlying the choices

Session Scriptures

Deuteronomy 18:10–14; Matthew 4:1–11; 1 Corinthians 2:12–16; Ephesians 2:1–3; Hebrews 1:1,2

Outline

   I. Finding the source
  II. Wrong ways to make choices
 III. Misleading formulas for making choices
     A. Relying on worldly common sense
     B. Using the closed-door policy
     C. Using the open-door policy
     D. Waiting for dramatic revelations

Leader's Preparation

How many times have you heard Christians say, "I just have a hunch that this is what I should do"? Or has someone remarked, "The door to this opportunity is closed, so that means God doesn't want me to take it"? How about this one? "God expects us to use our common sense, so I just think through all of my options before I decide."

These are just a few of the methods Christians use in trying to make the right choices in their lives. Are these methods correct or will they lead a person down the wrong path?

In this lesson, your students will discover several misleading formulas for discovering God's will. One, using occultic practices, is always wrong in God's eyes. Another, depending on emotions and feelings, is an unreliable method. The others have elements that we can use in decision-making, but are misleading when used exclusively.

Each of the formulas you will discuss in this session includes biblical examples. Before leading this session, study the examples used in the lesson:

- Elymas the sorcerer—Acts 13:6–12

- Believers who left the occult—Acts 19:18–20

- Peter rebuking Jesus—Matthew 16:21–23

- Jesus in the Garden of Gethsemane—Luke 22:39–44

- Solomon's wisdom—1 Kings 3:5–28; Ecclesiastes 1:13–18

- Joshua at the Jordan River—Joshua 3:13–17

- Paul going to Macedonia—Acts 16:6–10

- Abraham and Lot dividing up the land—Genesis 13:1–18; 19:12–17

- Philip meeting the Ethiopian eunuch—Acts 8:26–38

- The twelve apostles—Acts 6:1–7

These biblical accounts will form the backdrop for discussing how people make decisions and the results of the formulas they use.

The goal of this lesson is to help students examine methods they have been using to follow God's will. Because of the sensitive nature of this examination, guide the group into a time of private reflection during the Application. The purpose of the Action Point is not to determine whether or not the choices made were God's will. The purpose of the activity is to have group members discover how they arrived at their decisions and whether the method fits one of the misleading formulas.

As you lead the group into the prayer time, continue the reflective, quiet atmosphere. Allow the Holy Spirit to work among group members as they consider the importance of finding God's will. This should prepare them for Step 3 in which they commit themselves to following God's will.

The Bible Study Session

Sharing (3 minutes)

Ask students how their view of God has changed as a result of studying His attributes. Encourage volunteers to share how using praise during their quiet times helped them focus on God during the day.

Discussion Starter (7 minutes)

Say: Imagine that you are in this position:

The company you work for offers you a promotion, but it means transferring to a city a thousand miles away. The promotion includes a higher salary and better retirement benefits. If you do not take the promotion, you will be frozen in your position for the rest of your career in the company.

You have a teenage son who has been getting into minor trouble at school. When he hears about the move, he gets very upset.

You own a house, and selling it at this time means that you will probably take a loss. You also enjoy the leadership role you have at your church. You have good friends at work, in your neighborhood, and at church.

You check out the community in which you would locate and find that it has less crime than the area in which you now live. You also notice quite a few churches from which to choose.

Discuss: How will you decide what to do? Describe the steps you will take to make your decision.

Lesson Development (35–45 minutes)

Finding the Source

Say: One of the difficulties of discerning God's will is the influence of our human frailties. People often mistake God's leading with that of Satan's influence, worldly desires, or their own fleshly nature. If you read the newspaper, you can see extreme examples of this. People claim that God told them to bomb a building or commit murder. Others rationalize that God accepts whatever we do as long as we do it "in love."

We must know the source of leading before responding to it. To the inexperienced, what appears to be the leading of God's Spirit may not be from Him at all, but from other influences.

To help us avoid making decisions that do not follow godly principles, we must examine the source of our choices. The Bible says that there are three ways we are influenced to do the wrong thing: through satanic temptation, worldly persuasion, and fleshly desires. Let us look at a passage in Ephesians that describes these sources.

Read Ephesians 2:1–3. Then ask your students to turn to Lesson 2 in their Study Guides. Fill out the chart together.

Source	Description of the source	Result of following the source	How to handle the source
Flesh (sinful desires)	Galatians 5:19–21 *(See the list of fleshly desires.)*	Romans 8:5–8; Galatians 6:8 *(Death; hostility to God; cannot please God; destruction.)*	Romans 8:9; 1 Peter 2:11 *(Be controlled by the Spirit; stay away from sinful desires.)*
World	1 John 2:15–17 *(Everything in the world—sinful cravings, lust, boasting.)*	1 Corinthians 3:1–3; James 4:4 *(Spiritual immaturity, jealousy; quarreling; hatred toward God.)*	Romans 12:2 *(Don't be conformed to the world; be transformed by renewing your mind.)*
Satan	Ephesians 6:12 *(Rulers of darkness; powers of the dark world; spiritual forces of evil.)*	2 Corinthians 11:3; 1 Peter 5:8 *(Being led astray from devotion to Christ; Satan will defeat us.)*	James 4:7,8 *(Resist the devil; draw near to God; purify your hearts.)*

After you finish discussing the chart, say: As you have probably noticed, these sources overlap. Certainly the world tempts us with fleshly desires. Television ads are a good example of this. Our flesh makes us susceptible to the world's pleasures. For example, sensuality can lead us into a worldly lifestyle. And of course Satan uses our fleshly desires and the world's influence to defeat us.

Let us read the account of our Lord's temptation in the wilderness. It is not only an example of how to resist temptation, but of how to make godly choices. Jesus chose God's will. Let us look at how He made His choices.

Read Matthew 4:1–11. Ask:

- What fleshly desire did Jesus face? *(Hunger.)*

- What are some worldly pleasures that Jesus faced? *(Position of power; owning all the kingdoms of the world.)*

- How did Satan try to lure Jesus into sin? *(He promised to give Christ power over the world if He worshipped Satan; he appealed to Christ's pride by tempting Him to use His ability to perform miracles and to be protected by angels.)*

■ How did Jesus resist making wrong choices? *(He quoted God's Word correctly; He told Satan to leave; He refused to listen to Satan's suggestions.)*

Say: The Bible shows us how Jesus made correct choices in many different situations. In the Garden of Gethsemane, He chose to go to the cross rather than avoid pain and suffering. During His ministry, He chose to follow God's laws rather than succumb to the religious leaders' system of beliefs. He resisted Satan's influence when Peter rebuked Jesus for talking about His future death. Jesus recognized the sources trying to influence Him to make wrong choices, and He rejected them.

During the rest of our session, we will look at several formulas that we should reject because they could lead us into making wrong choices: ones that God condemns; ones that are unreliable; and ones that are wrong when used incorrectly.

Wrong Ways to Make Choices

Say: Some methods for making decisions are always wrong because they rely on influences other than God or His Word. If we rely on spiritual sources other than God's Spirit or rely on our emotions, feelings, or hunches, we will make wrong choices. Let's look more closely at each of these methods for making decisions, beginning with relying on other spiritual sources.

1. Occultic Practices

God is the only answer to our life. He is the One who rules the affairs of men and women. He is the One to whom we must go for direction in life. Any source other than Him will lead us into sin and death. That is why the Bible condemns searching for answers from other spiritual sources.

But we live in a society in which people are increasingly seeking advice from the powers of darkness through the occult. These methods replace our faith in God and open us up to satanic influence. God warns us strongly against using occultic practices. They include astrology, fortune-telling, occultic magic (not sleight-of-hand entertainment), using a medium, seeking omens or supernatural signs, numerology, palm reading, tarot cards, Ouija boards, clairvoyance, sorcery, and witchcraft. **Read Deuteronomy 18:10–14.** Satan and his helpers often disguise themselves as angels of light by foretelling events or performing miracles and signs. The enemy of our souls is a master counterfeiter.

As we know, we have access to the greatest power and wisdom in the universe. That power, which is available to help us make wise choices, is from God. When we base our decisions on His will, we will defeat Satan and his devious plans. To illustrate just how powerful God is, let me read a story about an African tribe who worshipped evil spirits and practiced occultic rituals. Although they were well acquainted with Satan's power, they also recognized a power greater than the one they worshipped. Dela Adadevoh, who directs the Campus Crusade work in Africa, tells what happened when one "JESUS" film team brought the Good News of Christ to these people. **Read:**

> The team went to an animistic tribe and, after they finished showing the "JESUS" film, the village leaders got together and began to question the film team. They asked, "Is your God more powerful than the sun god?"
>
> "Yes," the film team members answered.
>
> "Is Jesus more powerful than the god of the big trees?"
>
> A film team worker said, "Yes."
>
> "Is He more powerful than the witch doctors we have here?"
>
> "Yes, He is."
>
> "All right, then, we will decide to follow the God Jesus." And they cut down their big trees that they were worshiping, and burned their amulets and idols. They immediately formed three new churches, and after that two more. Today, each of the churches has more than 200 in attendance.

Satan and his evil spirits were not able to stop these people from receiving Christ as their Savior and forming new churches. In fact, God's power was so great that the churches kept growing.

Our God is more powerful than anything Satan can do. To avoid the dangers of spirit-worship, we need to avoid listening to or following spirits who are part of Satan's kingdom. Let us look at two examples of occultic practices from the New Testament. For each, we will list the decision made and its result. Turn to "Wrong Ways to Make Choices" in your Study Guide.

Read the verses, and encourage students to write down each decision and its result.

Elymas the sorcerer—Acts 13:6–12

> Decision: *(He tried to oppose God by keeping the proconsul from God's Word.)*

> Result: *(Elymas became blind; the proconsul believed in Jesus.)*

Many believers—Acts 19:18–20

> Decision: *(They turned away from their occultic practices.)*

> Result: *(The word of the Lord grew mightily.)*

2. Emotions, Feelings, or Hunches

Say: Another way many Christians make decisions is through their emotions, feelings, or hunches. Some sincere believers rely almost entirely upon hunches, fearful that if they use their mental faculties, they will not exercise adequate faith and thereby grieve the Holy Spirit. **Ask:**

- What may happen to the person who bases his decisions on feelings? *(He may change his mind later; he may not make a rational choice.)*

- Think of a time when you used one of these methods. What happened? *(Allow students to respond.)*

- Is taking your feelings into account wrong? Why? *(No, our feelings are important to acknowledge and consider, but should not be the sole basis for our decisions.)*

Say: Note the train diagram in your Study Guide. It illustrates the proper role of feelings in our decision-making. The facts about God and His Word are the engine or the power in our lives. Faith in God and our obedience are the fuel that puts God's will into action. Our feelings follow as a result of our obedience to God's will by faith. We would no more run our lives by feelings than we would attempt to pull a train by the caboose. A Christian's faith is built on the authority of God's Word and not on shallow experiences. God considers our desires and feelings important, but He does not want us to follow our unreliable, shifting emotions or use hunches to make our decisions.

Let us look at two examples of people who made choices where emotions were involved.

Peter—Matthew 16:21–23

> Decision: *(Peter impulsively rebuked Jesus because he felt that Jesus was wrong when He began teaching about His impending death on the cross.)*

> Result: *(Peter was rebuked by Jesus, who said Satan was using Peter as a stumbling block to God's interests.)*

Jesus—Luke 22:39–44

> Decision: *(In spite of strong feelings, Jesus submitted to God's will and was willing to endure the crucifixion.)*

> Result: *(We obtained eternal life through His death and resurrection.)*

Say: This is the supreme example of putting feelings aside to make the right choice. Can you imagine the ending to world history if Jesus had let His feelings dictate His choice? Many times, our feelings will influence us to take the easy way out, but when we obey God's will, our feelings usually fall in line. Feelings change, but the facts of God's Word are unchanging.

Misleading Formulas for Making Choices

Through the centuries, sincere religious people have used many popular formulas for discovering the will of God. Some are valid; others are unscriptural and misleading. These formulas contain elements of truth for discerning God's plan, but if we apply them to the exclusion of other vital considerations, they do not give us a complete picture of how God is working through a particular situation. By examining these formulas, we can see how they may mislead even sincere Christians.

1. Relying on Worldly Common Sense

There is a vast difference between the "wisdom" of the natural man (an unbeliever) or the worldly Christian and the wisdom of the spiritual person who follows the principles in God's Word. The natural man relies on all kinds of knowledge that can sometimes be harmful. He is swayed by the general thinking of the day. For example, a popular belief today is that living together outside marriage helps a couple get to know each other before they make a permanent commitment through marriage. On the surface, there seems to be some logic in this view. But God says that premarital sex is wrong. And statistics show that couples who lived together before marriage have a higher divorce rate than couples who did not. In this case, worldly common sense leads to a wrong conclusion that can have disastrous results.

Of course, God has given us a mind to use, and acting on common sense is part of our responsibility. But we must always submit our common sense to the truth in God's Word. Where we go wrong is in making common-sense decisions without checking them against the principles and commands in God's Word. Relying on worldly common sense means depending on the wisdom of man for understanding without receiving the benefit of God's infinite wisdom and power, and is therefore a misleading formula. But the person who has the mind of Christ receives wisdom from God through his faith and obedience.

Read 1 Corinthians 2:12–16, then discuss the following questions:

- What do you think is the difference between having worldly common sense and having the mind of Christ? *(The source of worldly common sense is the world, but the source of the mind of Christ is God's Spirit living in us; common sense fluctuates with situations and culture, but the person who has the mind of Christ is stable in his thinking.)*

■ How, then, might relying completely on a worldly type of common sense affect a person's decision-making? *(Decisions may not be true to biblical principles; a person may think something is wise just because a lot of other people think the same way; it is easy to make wrong choices and not even realize it.)*

Say: The examples of using godly and worldly wisdom come from Solomon's experiences. Read the Bible passages under "Relying on Worldly Common Sense" in your Study Guides, and give the decision and result. Then we will discuss the answers. **Give students time to write, then discuss.**

Solomon—1 Kings 3:5–28

Decision: *(Solomon asked God for wisdom to judge the people.)*

Result: *(Solomon administered justice and his people realized that his wisdom in decision-making came from God.)*

Solomon—Ecclesiastes 1:13–18

Decision: *(Later in life, Solomon searched for the world's knowledge and lived his life by it.)*

Result: *(He met only pain and discouragement in the world's wisdom.)*

Say: Just like many of us, Solomon started out by relying on God for wisdom. As he grew older, he lost his first love for the Lord and let worldly pleasures and desires replace his devotion to God. As a result, he became disillusioned and discouraged.

That is where relying on worldly common sense and neglecting God's wisdom eventually lead us. God does want us to use common sense, as Solomon did when he judged between the two women. But God wants our reasoning to be rooted in His Word and to be led by His Spirit. In a later Step, we will learn how we can use good sense that follows biblical principles.

2. Using the Closed-Door Policy

Say: The closed-door policy consists of making decisions by turning away from opportunities that may be blocked. Bill Bright, who has written this curriculum and is co-founder and president of Campus Crusade for Christ, gives this example:

> A young seminary graduate came to see me. He was investigating various possibilities for Christian service and had come to discuss the ministry of Campus Crusade for Christ. I asked him, "In what way do you expect God to reveal His place of service to you?"
>
> He replied, "I'm following the closed-door policy. A few months ago, I began to investigate several opportunities for Christian service. The Lord has now closed the door on all but two, and Campus Crusade for Christ is one. If the door to accept a call to the other opportunity closes, I will know that God wants me in Campus Crusade."
>
> I did not hear from him after our meeting. I assume that he considered the "door" to join Campus Crusade for Christ was also closed when I explained to him that following the closed-door policy was not a good way to discover God's choice.

Ask:

- What do you think is wrong with relying on this formula for decision-making? *(Perhaps God did not close the door; the door may seem to be closed when God wants to miraculously send you in that direction.)*

Say: Many Christians follow the illogical and unbiblical closed-door policy, often with unsatisfactory and frustrating consequences. Don't misunderstand. God may and often does close and open doors in the life of an active, Spirit-filled Christian. God's work in our lives does not exclude such experiences, but the closed-door policy refers to a careless hit-or-miss attitude that does not include careful evaluation of all the issues. Let us look at two biblical examples of the closed-door policy. **Give students time to fill out the questions in their Study Guides, then discuss their answers.**

Joshua and the Israelites—Joshua 3:13–17

Decision: *(To enter the Promised Land, Joshua and his people had to go against logic and choose to set foot in the flooding Jordan River to cross as God commanded them.)*

Result: *(As soon as the priests stepped out in faith and their feet touched the water, God parted the river and the people all walked across on dry ground.)*

Paul—Acts 16:6–10

Decision: *(Following God's command, Paul did not go to Bithynia as he had intended.)*

Result: *(God sent Paul to instead minister in Macedonia where the harvest was ripe.)*

Say: Why is relying exclusively on the closed-door policy misleading? Because it allows elements of chance to influence a decision rather than you carefully, intelligently evaluate all the factors involved and seek God's leading. The closed-door policy is unbiblical because it fails to employ the God-given faculties of reason, which are controlled by the Holy Spirit. Further, the closed-door policy is open to error because it seeks God's will through a process of elimination instead of seeking God's best first. As the train diagram illustrates, true faith is established on fact—the truth of God's Word. Therefore, we should emphasize vital faith in God through relying on Spirit-controlled reason rather than emphasizing circumstances such as closed doors.

Some Christians assume that a door is closed simply because of difficulties. One question logically follows: How do we know whether God is closing the door or whether we are encountering opposition from Satan, the world, or our fleshly nature? Experience and God's Word will confirm that God's richest blessings often follow periods of great testing. This might include financial needs, loss of health, or criticism from a loved one.

Ask:

- How have you seen God use difficulties to bring blessing in your life? (Allow for responses.)

Then say: Every significant effort for the Lord will entail major—sometimes overwhelming—problems and resistance. God promises His blessings to those who are obedient to His will, who keep on trusting, and who demonstrate active faith in Him no matter how difficult circumstances appear. The greatest example of this truth? Christ's seeming "defeat" by death on the cross was followed by the victory of the resurrection!

3. Using the Open-Door Policy

Say: The principles for misusing the closed-door policy also apply to the open-door policy. Through this method, a person selects the easiest path as God's will. Christians who use this method rationalize, "If the door to this opportunity is open, then God must want me to go through it." They do not realize that Satan may sometimes use open doors to tempt us away from God's best. **Give students time to answer the questions in the Study Guides. Then discuss their responses.**

Lot and Abraham—Genesis 13:1–18; 19:12–17

Decision: *(Lot chose the pleasant land in the valley near the wicked city of Sodom; remembering that God had promised to bless him, Abraham was content to settle on the less productive land.)*

Result: *(Lot became entangled in the wicked culture of the cities and lost everything he owned when God destroyed Sodom for its wickedness.)*

Paul and Silas—Acts 16:23–34

Decision: *(Paul and Silas decided to remain in their prison cell after an earthquake opened all the doors and loosed the stocks around their legs.)*

Result: *(Their decision kept the jailer from taking his own life and gained the opportunity to introduce him and his family to Christ.)*

Say: As we have seen through these examples, an open door does not necessarily mean that it is God's will. What a tragedy might have occurred if Paul and Silas had immediately escaped from prison after the earthquake. But they were walking closely with the Lord and understood His will in their difficult situation. They kept their eyes on the goal of winning others to Christ, not just on their personal comfort and safety. How can we approach a situation when an open door presents itself suddenly? We can consider it as another opportunity for us to bring our decision before God and to influence His kingdom.

Ask:

- How has God used open doors to lead you? *(Allow for responses.)*
- On the other hand, what open doors have you encountered that were not God's will? *(Allow for responses.)*

Say: Open doors may be misleading or they may be God's way of guiding us into His will. In a later Step, we will learn how to recognize the doors that God opens.

4. Waiting for Dramatic Revelations

Say: Many Christians wait for some dramatic revelation from God to know His plan. They want visual proof of something that is usually determined by faith. That reasoning, when carried to extremes, can cause us real problems. Although there are exceptions, God's communication to us is seldom dramatic.

Author Elisabeth Elliot explains in *A Slow and Certain Light:*

> There is one thing we ought to notice about [biblical] miracles. When God guided by means of the pillar of cloud and fire, by the star of Bethlehem, by visitations of angels, by the word coming through visions and dreams and prophets and even through an insulted donkey, in most cases these were not signs that had been asked for. And when they were asked for, as in the case of Jehoshaphat and Ahab, they were not accepted.
>
> Supernatural phenomena were given at the discretion of the divine wisdom. It is not for us to ask that God will guide us in

some miraculous way. If, in His wisdom, He knows that such means are what we need, He will surely give them.[3]

Today, God speaks to us through the example of His Son. **Read Hebrews 1:1,2.** God still reveals His will to some men and women in dramatic ways, but this is the exception rather than the rule. Let us look at examples of this leading. **Give students time to complete this section of their Study Guides.**

Philip—Acts 8:26–38

> Decision: *(During Philip's preaching ministry, God sent an angel to tell him to take a certain road. On that road, he met the Ethiopian eunuch whom God had prepared to receive Philip's message of God's love and forgiveness.)*

> Result: *(Philip obeyed God's revelation, and through his witness the eunuch became a Christian and took his faith back to his country.)*

The twelve apostles—Acts 6:1–7

> Decision: *(Faced with a decision on how to meet the needs of the Greek widows and still preach the Word of God, the apostles chose to select godly men to take responsibility for food distribution. Their decision was based on logical thinking rather than a direct revelation from God.)*

> Result: *(The apostles were able to spend their time preaching and the equitable treatment of the widows became a witness to the community. As a result, the Word of God spread rapidly.)*

Say: In the first example, God sent an angel to Philip with detailed directions on how to proceed with his ministry. In the second example, the apostles decided as a group to appoint others to share in the responsibilities. The apostles used Spirit-controlled wisdom to select godly men. God did not give them special revelation.

---

[3] Elisabeth Elliot, *A Slow and Certain Light: Some Thoughts on the Guidance of God*, Waco, TX: Word Books, 1973, pp. 85, 86.

God does not tell us to wait for a divine revelation before we act. He wants us to follow His will for momentous decisions and for daily choices. Communion with Jesus Christ, obedience to His commands, and trusting His Spirit result in discovering God's will.

In the next three Steps, we will learn how to apply God's will to our lives. To do so, we will not use a formula, but will study the Sound Mind Principle of God's Word.

But before we close our session today, let us examine a few decisions in the past week to see if we have been using any misleading formulas.

Application (5 minutes)

Give students time to complete the chart in the Action Point. Do not discuss the answers as a group. Ask: Now that you have filled out the chart, have your decisions changed in any way?

Closing and Prayer (5 minutes)

Encourage your students to examine their upcoming decisions according to the information they learned in this lesson. Then close by thanking God for His loving attention to our daily lives and our big decisions.

Follow-Up

During the time before your next session, be sensitive to helping students who are facing important decisions. Resist the urge to give advice, but direct them to appropriate Bible passages and pray with them.

At this point in your study group, encourage your students to share the good news of what they are learning about God's will with their friends who may be interested in joining a similar Bible study.

Student Lesson Plan

Finding the Source

To the inexperienced, what appears to be the leading of God's Holy Spirit may not be from Him at all, but from other influences. Therefore, we must know the source of leading before responding to it.

The Bible says that there are three ways we are influenced to do the wrong thing: through satanic temptation, worldly persuasion, and fleshly desires.

Read Ephesians 2:1–3 then fill out the chart.

Source	Description of the source	Result of following the source	How to handle the source
Flesh (sinful desires)	Galatians 5:19–21	Romans 8:5–8; Galatians 6:8	Romans 8:9; 1 Peter 2:11
World	1 John 2:15–17	1 Corinthians 3:1–3; James 4:4	Romans 12:2
Satan	Ephesians 6:12	2 Corinthians 11:3; 1 Peter 5:8	James 4:7,8

Our Lord's temptation in the wilderness is an example of how to make godly choices. Jesus chose to follow God's will. Read Matthew 4:1–11 and answer the questions.

- What fleshly desire did Jesus face?

- What are some worldly pleasures that Jesus faced?

- How did Satan try to lure Jesus into sin?
- How did Jesus resist making wrong choices?

Wrong Ways to Make Choices

Occultic Practices

God warns us strongly against using occultic practices. They include astrology, fortune-telling, occultic magic (not sleight-of-hand entertainment), using a medium, seeking omens or supernatural signs, numerology, palm reading, tarot cards, Ouija boards, clairvoyance, sorcery, and witchcraft (Deuteronomy 18:10–14).

Read the following verses, and write down each decision and its result.

Elymas the sorcerer—Acts 13:6–12

    Decision:

    Result:

Many believers—Acts 19:18–20

    Decision:

    Result:

Emotions, Feelings, or Hunches

This train diagram illustrates the proper role of feelings in our decision-making. The facts about God and His Word are the engine or the power in our lives. Faith in God and our obedience are the fuel that puts God's will into action. Our feelings follow as a result of our obedience to God's will by faith. We would no more run our lives by feelings than we would attempt to pull a train by the caboose.

Read the following verses, and write down each decision and its result.

Peter—Matthew 16:21–23

Decision:

Result:

Jesus—Luke 22:39–44

Decision:

Result:

Misleading Formulas for Making Choices

Through the centuries, sincere religious people have used many popular formulas for discovering the will of God. Some are valid; others are unscriptural and misleading. These formulas contain elements of truth for discerning God's plan, but if we apply them to the exclusion of other vital considerations, they do not give us a complete picture of how God is working through a particular situation.

1. Relying on Worldly Common Sense

God has given us a mind to use, but we must always submit our common sense to the truth in God's Word. Relying on worldly common sense means depending on the wisdom of man for understanding without receiving the benefit of God's infinite wisdom and power.

Read the verses, and write down each decision and result.

Solomon—1 Kings 3:5–28

Decision:

Result:

Solomon—Ecclesiastes 1:13–18

Decision:

Result:

2. Using the Closed-Door Policy

The closed-door policy consists of making decisions by turning away from opportunities that may be blocked.

Read the verses, and write the decision and result for each situation.

Joshua and the Israelites—Joshua 3:13–17

Decision:

Result:

Paul—Acts 16:6–10

Decision:

Result:

Every significant effort for the Lord will entail major—sometimes overwhelming—problems and resistance. God promises His blessings to those who are obedient to His will, who keep on trusting, and who demonstrate active faith in Him no matter how difficult circumstances appear. The greatest example of this truth? Christ's seeming "defeat" by death on the cross was followed by the victory of the resurrection!

3. Using the Open-Door Policy

Through this method, a person selects the easiest path as God's will. Christians who use this method rationalize, "If the door to this opportunity is open, then God must want me to go through it." They do not realize that Satan may sometimes use open doors to tempt us away from God's best.

After reading the verses, give the decision and result for each situation.

Lot and Abraham—Genesis 13:1–18; 19:12–17

Decision:

Result:

Paul and Silas—Acts 16:23–34

  Decision:

  Result:

4. *Waiting for Dramatic Revelations*

Many Christians want visual proof of something that is usually determined by faith. Although there are exceptions, God's communication to us today is seldom dramatic or unusual.

Read the verses and write down the decision and result.

Philip—Acts 8:26–38

  Decision:

  Result:

The twelve apostles—Acts 6:1–7

  Decision:

  Result:

Action Point: Using this chart, examine two of the decisions you have made in the past month.

Decision I made	Questions to ask	Result of the decision
	1. Did I use any of the methods mentioned in this lesson? 2. How did I apply these methods? 3. In what way did I check my decision against the principles in God's Word?	
	1. Did I use any of the methods mentioned in this lesson? 2. How did I apply these methods? 3. In what way did I check my decision against the principles in God's Word?	

STEP 3

Discover the Sound Mind Principle

Focus

The Sound Mind Principle of Scripture allows a Spirit-filled Christian to make decisions based on the biblical guidelines found in 2 Timothy 1:7 and Romans 12:1,2.

Objectives

This session will help students to:

- *Learn* the definition of the Sound Mind Principle

- *Discover* how to renew their minds according to Romans 12:1,2

- *Examine* daily activities in light of the heart of Christ's mission

- *Commit* themselves to following Christ and walking in the Spirit

Session Scriptures

Psalm 37:23; Matthew 28:18–20; Luke 19:10; John 15:1–5,8; Romans 1:17; 12:1,2; 14:23; 1 Corinthians 2:14–16; Ephesians 5:18; 2 Timothy 1:7; Hebrews 11:6; 1 John 1:9; 15:14,15

Outline

   I. The Sound Mind Principle
  II. The mind of Christ
 III. Contributing to Christ's mission
 IV. Faith is the key

V. Factors for using the Sound Mind Principle
   A. There must be no unconfessed sin.
   B. Your life must be dedicated to Christ and you must be filled with the Spirit.
   C. You must walk in the Spirit.

Leader's Preparation

The book of 2 Timothy, from which the Sound Mind Principle is taken, was written to leaders of the early church. These leaders were commanded to shepherd Christ's sheep and guard them against false teachers. Timothy, a dedicated young man, had been given the responsibility of pastoring the church in Ephesus. He had spent many months traveling with the apostle Paul who taught him how to live a godly life and guide new believers. Now it was Timothy's turn to put into practice what he had learned. In this letter, Paul was writing to Timothy, giving him more detailed instructions on how to be a godly leader.

Who needs more guidance in making decisions than those in charge of the spiritual life of the church? This was certainly true in the first centuries of the Church. In addition to the persecution and the pagan culture that oppressed the Christians after Christ's resurrection, false teachers had sprung up within their midst. Always practical, Paul wanted Timothy to not only learn doctrine, but also apply it to his life and teach it to his flock. Second Timothy 1:7 gives the basic principle of how to make decisions according to God's plan.

The wisdom that Paul passed on to Timothy we can apply to our lives too. By linking 2 Timothy 1:7 to Romans 12:1,2, your students can begin to apply the Sound Mind Principle to their lives. As you guide this session, emphasize that Christ's mission to seek and save the lost is our priority in life. Each of our decisions should reflect His desire for everyone to know Him as Savior and Lord.

Help students learn the importance of their commitment to Christ's mission by modeling its priority in your life and by encouraging your students to witness as a way of life. To receive more practical help in witnessing, you can obtain *Five Steps to Sharing Your Faith*, a Bible study that gives step-by-step instruction on how to introduce a person to Jesus Christ.

Bring your flip chart to this session.

The Bible Study Session

Sharing (5 minutes)

Recap the previous lesson by saying: During our last session, we looked at some wrong and misleading formulas for making choices. These formulas are:

- Searching for answers through occultic practices

- Depending on emotions, feelings, or hunches

- Relying on worldly common sense

- Practicing a closed-door policy

- Using an open-door policy

- Waiting for dramatic revelations

Then discuss: For many people, the most difficult time to make a decision is during an urgent situation. Which one of these formulas are you tempted to turn to whenever you face an urgent decision? Why?

Discussion Starter (7 minutes)

Say: Today we are going to talk about how to discover God's will in all kinds of situations. To get us started, I want to read a true story. **Read:**

> Once a week, a discipleship group of 50 to 80 men met at a church early in the morning. Before breaking into smaller groups for study, Peter, the group leader, led a sharing time. One morning, a tall, muscular man about 50 years of age stood and gave a testimony.
>
> "I was in the process of deciding whether or not to make a major career move," he explained, "but I just didn't know what God wanted me to do.

Then Peter gave me a copy of the Paul Brown Letter.[4] In it, I read about something called the Sound Mind Principle. I had never heard of it before.

"I went through the principle and applied it to my decision about a job change. By the time I finished, it was clear to me that God didn't want me to change positions.

"Now that I've made the decision and lived with it for a while, I'm so thankful that I didn't make the career move! God saved me from making a bad decision that I may have regretted for many years."

Say: In this session, we will discover the definition of the Sound Mind Principle, read Scriptures that give the basics of the principle, and consider factors in applying its concepts. In the following two sessions, we will look at the remainder of the principle and learn how to apply it to any decision we might face.

But first, let us talk about the bottom line in decision making. **Ask:**

- What do you think are the most important factors to consider when making any decision? *(Allow for responses.)*

As students give responses, write them on your flip chart. Then ask:

- What are the most prevalent ideas in these suggestions? *(Allow for responses.)*

Say: As we look at the Sound Mind Principle in this lesson, we can see if any of our responses fit into good decision-making.

Lesson Development (40 minutes)

The Sound Mind Principle

Say: As we learned in the last session, finding God's will can sometimes seem like a difficult task. Yet knowing the attributes of God and His faithfulness and what He wants us to do with our

---

[4] The Paul Brown Letter gave the original Sound Mind Principle and was used for many years as a tool in decision-making. Copies are available from New*Life* Publications at (800) 235-7255.

lives is absolutely one of the most important parts of our Christian walk.

How can we firmly discern God's will for our lives? While most of God's will is revealed in Scripture, the Bible also gives us a principle for discerning His will in matters not addressed by direct command. Called the Sound Mind Principle of Scripture, it has helped many Christians discover God's will. Dr. Bill Bright gives this illustration. **Read:**

> During one of my speaking engagements at Wheaton College, a senior by the name of Jim Green approached me and said, "I don't know what God wants me to do with my life, and I need to talk to you."
>
> Jim was a gifted person and could have pursued a career in several fields. I said, "The safest approach to knowing God's will is to follow what I call the Sound Mind Principle of Scripture. This principle applies biblical truths to decision making." Briefly, I explained the principle to him, then hurried off to another appointment.
>
> When I saw Jim later that afternoon, he was very excited. "Not only has God shown me what He wants me to do, but He has shown me the organization He wants me to be associated with!" In less than an hour, by using the Sound Mind Principle, this young man discovered what he had been seeking for years.
>
> Jim and his wife, Nan, have faithfully and fruitfully served our Lord on our staff in both English- and French-speaking African countries. I wrote the Paul Brown Letter as a result of my experience with my beloved friend.

Say: Does this sound too easy? Not every decision can be made this quickly, but the Sound Mind Principle does give specific guidance on how to seek the mind of God. The basics of the Sound Mind Principle are found in 2 Timothy 1:7.

Read 2 Timothy 1:7: "God has not given us a spirit of fear, but of power and of love and of a sound mind" (NKJ). **Then say:** Your Study Guide gives a definition of the Sound Mind Principle. **Invite a volunteer to read the definition:**

The Sound Mind Principle of 2 Timothy 1:7 means a well-balanced mind that is under the control of the Holy Spirit, transformed according to Romans 12:1,2.

Say: The Greek term "sound mind" can also be translated as "discipline." The idea of discipline in this context means "the power to make godly choices in the face of other alternatives." Having a sound mind means that our thought process is being transformed through the power of the Holy Spirit.

Christians with a sound mind receive wisdom and guidance from God by faith. In contrast, dependence on man's wisdom will lead us away from God's best for us because it is based on self-interest and an undue emphasis on emotions or chance circumstances. **Ask:**

- How is having a sound mind different than relying on worldly common sense? *(A sound mind is disciplined and dependent on God's Word, whereas depending too heavily on worldly common sense may result in a spur-of-the-moment decision; a sound mind is under the control of the Holy Spirit, whereas worldly common sense stems from the world's wisdom.)*

- How is having a sound mind different than relying on emotions, feelings, or hunches? *(A sound mind relies on God and His Word, not ourselves; a sound mind comes from the work of the Holy Spirit in our lives, not from our changing feelings.)*

Say: The first step, then, is to follow the command in James 1:5–8 and ask for wisdom. **Read these verses.** Only God can give us the wisdom to make the right choices, and faith is the channel that opens our minds and hearts to God's wisdom. Our faith allows us to begin thinking like Christ.

The Mind of Christ

Say: The definition of the Sound Mind Principle refers to Romans 12:1,2. This passage will help us apply the Sound Mind Principle. **Read Romans 12:1,2. Ask:**

- What do you think it means to be a living sacrifice? *(Allow for responses.)*

- Why do you think we cannot discern God's will unless our minds are renewed or transformed? *(When we think like the world, we cannot know God's thoughts unless we let Him change our minds to reflect His attitudes.)*

Say: Romans 12:1,2 includes a two-part commitment to do God's will. Reread the verses and fill out the two points under "The Mind of Christ" in your Study Guide as we look at them together. **Encourage students to write the following two points in their Study Guides as you write them on your flip chart.**

1. Romans 12:1: We must commit to obeying God's will as He reveals it.

2. Romans 12:2: We must turn from the world's ways and allow God to transform us.

Discuss the following question, and ask students to write their answers in the Study Guide:

- Why are each of these parts so important? *(Our commitment allows God to reveal His will to us; if we follow the world's system of beliefs, we will miss God's will for our lives.)*

Then read 1 Corinthians 2:14–16. Say: Having the mind of Christ means thinking like He thinks and having the same priorities He does. Jesus had specific reasons for coming to Earth in human form and submitting to death by crucifixion. To know the will of God for our lives according to the Sound Mind Principle of Scripture, we can follow the logic contained in the next three questions, which reflect the heart of Christ's mission.

Ask students to privately answer the three questions under "The Mind of Christ" in the Study Guide. Then go over the questions as a group, making sure that the answers given below are emphasized.

1. Why did Jesus come to Earth (Luke 19:10)? *(To seek and save the lost.)*

2. What is the greatest experience of your life? *(To know Christ personally as my Savior and Lord.)*

3. Then what is the greatest thing you can do to help others? *(Introduce them to Christ.)*

Say: Christ's mission was to seek and save the lost, so every Christian is under divine orders to be a faithful witness for Him. **Read John 15:8. Say:** It logically follows that the most important thing we can possibly do as Christians is to allow the Lord Jesus Christ—in all of His resurrection power—to have complete, unhindered control of our life. Otherwise, He cannot continue seeking and saving the lost through us.

To focus our thoughts on Christ's priorities, these three questions are the first issue we must examine when making decisions. We consider how our choices can help us best contribute to seeking and saving the lost.

Just before He went back to heaven after His resurrection, Jesus commanded us to reach all people with God's message of love and forgiveness. **Read Matthew 28:18–20.** This is called the Great Commission.

To help us base decisions on our ability to introduce others to Jesus Christ or help fulfill the Great Commission, let us examine what we are doing right now in light of these three questions.

Contributing to Christ's Mission

Say: In your Study Guide you will find a chart called "My Contribution to Christ's Mission." Take a few minutes to think through your daily schedule. Write down all the major activities you have in your schedule, then fill out the questions for each activity. I will give you a few minutes to complete the chart.

When most students are finished, say: Now think about how you could be more effective in reflecting Christ's mission.

Under the chart, jot down any changes you need to make in your schedule that will help you become more effective in introducing others to Jesus Christ.

Give students another few moments to think and write.

My Contribution to Christ's Mission		
Activities in my schedule	**How am I reflecting Christ's mission in this activity?**	**What could I do to better reflect Christ's mission in this activity?**
(Example: going to the gym)	*(I am patient about using the equipment and am friendly to the other patrons.)*	*(I could use opportunities to talk to others as openings to share my faith.)*
These are the changes I will make in my activities to help me become more effective as a witness for Christ:		

Then say: In a similar way, we can apply the three questions that reflect the heart of Christ's mission to options we may have in making decisions. Let us discuss a few examples. In these hypothetical situations, there are no right or wrong answers. But we can come up with options that we might consider in similar circumstances. **Discuss the following two examples as a**

group, coming up with options each couple may consider. On your flip chart, write the options your students suggest.

Cheryl and Greg are considering buying a house. Although the homes they have looked at will mean higher payments than the rent they pay now, the amount is well within their budget. What factors might they consider in light of their commitment to share Christ with their neighbors? Base your comments on living situations you have experienced in the past or on likely scenarios for communities in our area.

Cassie and Chuck have three children. Now that the oldest is reaching school age, Cassie the Chuck are considering three options: home schooling, Christian school, or public school. Considering the three questions about Christ's mission, what are the pros and cons of each option? In your discussion, keep in mind that decisions like these are very personal and individually directed by God, so consider all three options as possibilities, even if your personal convictions may already be decided.

Say: Now we come to the key for implementing our decisions—our faith.

Faith Is the Key

Say: Faith is the channel that opens our minds and hearts to God's wisdom. In fact, faith is the catalyst for all of our Christian relationships and decisions. Colossians 2:6 says, "So then, just as you received Christ Jesus as Lord, continue to live in him." How did you receive Him? By faith, placing your complete trust in Him. Then continue walking by faith as a daily lifestyle. We can place our faith in the Lord that He is directing our steps and will continue to direct our lives, as He promised: **Read Psalm 37:23.**

Let us look at three verses that will help us understand the importance of faith. For each verse, write down the central truth about faith. **Give students time to write their answers in their Study Guides. Then briefly discuss the answers.**

- Romans 14:23 (*Everything that does not come from faith is sin.*)

- Romans 1:17 (*The just shall life by faith.*)

- Hebrews 11:6 *(Without faith it is impossible to please God.)*

Application (8 minutes)

Factors for Using the Sound Mind Principle

Say: Through the Sound Mind Principle, we receive wisdom and guidance from God moment by moment through faith. However, the Sound Mind Principle is not valid unless certain factors exist. Turn to the second chart in your Study Guide, and we will examine these factors.

Write the factors on your flip chart, read the verses, then discuss the questions following each factor.

1. There must be no unconfessed sin in your life (1 John 1:9).

   - Why is confession the first step in knowing God's will? *(Sin will blind us to God's will; sin inhibits us from making good choices; we cannot have fellowship with God and keep on sinning.)*

Encourage students to ask God to reveal any sin in their lives and to confess the sins that He brings to mind. Give them a few minutes of silent reflection to do this.

2. Your life must be fully dedicated to Christ, and you must be filled with and directed by the Holy Spirit (Romans 12:1,2 and Ephesians 5:18).

   - What will happen to our decision-making process if we are not fully committed to following Christ? *(We will rely on ourselves to make our own decisions; we will not be focused on what God wants for us.)*

Say: Let us take a moment of quiet reflection and prayer to examine our dedication to our wonderful Lord Jesus. Perhaps you have never given Him control of every part of your life. I urge you to prayerfully take that step right now. Or maybe you need to confirm or renew a commitment to Him that you have already made. I will give you a few moments to take this very important step.

Pause to give students time to pray. As they reflect, renew your own commitment to Christ. When students finish, say: As Ephesians 5:18 points out, an essential part of our commitment to Christ is to be filled with the Spirit. Being filled with the Holy Spirit means asking Him to control every attitude, motive, desire, thought, and action, allowing Him to work through you to do God's will.

Just as you received Christ by faith as a new believer, you are filled with the Holy Spirit by faith. In Ephesians 5:18, God *commands* us to be filled with His Spirit. In 1 John 5:14,15, God *promises* to answer any request that is in accordance with His will. **Read 1 John 5:14,15.** Since it is God's will for you to be filled with the Spirit and since He promises to answer any request that is according to His will, right now, as an act of your will by faith, ask God to fill you with His Spirit. If you are absolutely sure that you are filled with the Holy Spirit, pause to thank Him for filling you and invite Him to continue to do so. **Give students a few moments to pray. Then go on to the third point.**

3. To know the will of God, you must walk in the Spirit moment by moment. This is called abiding in Christ. **Read John 15:1–5, then ask:**

   ■ How does the relationship between a vine and branch picture our life in Christ? *(We get our spiritual life from Christ in the same way a branch gets life-giving nutrients from the vine. Just as a branch cannot grow unless it is attached to the vine, we cannot grow spiritually unless we abide in Christ.)*

   ■ How have you seen this principle work in your life in a specific situation or during a difficult problem? *(Encourage volunteers to describe how God's power, His Word, or fervent prayer has helped change a situation. Give an example of your own.)*

   ■ Now contrast this experience with a time when you acted on your own outside the wisdom and power of God. How were the results different? *(Allow for responses.)*

Closing and Prayer (5 minutes)

Say: In our next session, we will begin looking at our individual choices in situations we face. We will be answering questions such as, "How can we know for certain what God's will is?" and, "How does God communicate His will to us?"

Close by asking God to help group members apply the steps of change they noted in their Study Guides. Pray for any concerns the students mention. Then close by thanking God for having a heart for sinners and for adopting us into His family and giving us the opportunity to be His representatives to those who do not know Him.

Follow-Up

Plan individual time with each of your students over the next two sessions. During this time, talk about decisions they are facing and situations in which they want to know God's will. Encourage them to walk in the Spirit daily and to follow through with the changes they noted in their Study Guides. Also encourage students to prayerfully consider starting a study of their own.

Student Lesson Plan

The Sound Mind Principle

Finding God's will can sometimes seem like a difficult task. Yet knowing the attributes of God and His faithfulness and what He wants us to do with our lives is absolutely one of the most important parts of our Christian walk. To follow God's will means experiencing joy, peace, and fruitfulness and bringing glory to God.

Definition:

The Sound Mind Principle of 2 Timothy 1:7 means a well-balanced mind that is under the control of the Holy Spirit, transformed according to Romans 12:1,2.

- How is having a sound mind different than relying on worldly common sense?

- How is having a sound mind different than relying on emotions, feelings, or hunches?

The Mind of Christ

Romans 12:1,2 tells us how to seek God's will. In these verses, we find the two parts to our commitment.

1. Romans 12:1:

2. Romans 12:2:

- Why are each of these parts so important?

Read 1 Corinthians 2:14–16. Having the mind of Christ means thinking like He thinks and having the same priorities He does. These three questions reflect the heart of Christ's mission.

1. Why did Jesus come to Earth (Luke 19:10)?

2. What is the greatest experience of your life?

3. Then what is the greatest thing you can do to help others?

Contributing to Christ's Mission

Take a few minutes to think through your daily schedule. Write down all the major activities you have in your schedule, then fill out the chart for each activity. Consider how you could be more effective in reflecting Christ's mission.

My Contribution to Christ's Mission		
Activities in my schedule	How am I reflecting Christ's mission in this activity?	What could I do to better reflect Christ's mission in this activity?
(Example: going to the gym)	(I am patient about using the equipment and am friendly to the other patrons.)	(I could use opportunities to talk to others as openings to share my faith.)

These are the changes I will make in my activities to help me become more effective as a witness for Christ:

Faith Is the Key

Faith is the catalyst for all of our Christian relationships and decisions. Look at these verses and write down the central truth about faith:

Romans 14:23

Romans 1:17

Hebrews 11:6

Factors for Using the Sound Mind Principle

Through the Sound Mind Principle, we receive wisdom and guidance from God. But the principle is not valid unless these three factors exist. Consider these three factors in light of your decision-making.

1. *There must be no unconfessed sin in your life.* Follow the pattern in 1 John 1:9 to confess your sin.
2. *Your life must be fully dedicated to Christ, and you must be filled with and directed by the Holy Spirit* in obedience to Ephesians 5:18. We are filled and controlled by the Spirit through faith.
3. *You must walk in the Spirit moment by moment.* We continue abiding in Christ and trusting Him with our decisions.

Read John 15:1–5. Reflect on the following questions:

- How does the relationship between a vine and branch picture our life in Christ?

- How have you seen this principle work in your life in a specific situation or during a difficult problem?

- Now contrast this experience with a time when you acted on your own outside the wisdom and power of God. How were the results different?

STEP 4

Examine Your Options

Focus

To examine the options in a decision, we ask God to reveal His will, consult His Word, consider godly counsel, and "listen" to the Holy Spirit.

Objectives

This session will help students to:

- *Examine* their talents in light of the Great Commission
- *Choose* one decision to consider during the lesson
- *List* the options in the decision
- *Fill* out a Pro/Con Chart

Session Scriptures

Genesis 50:18–20; Psalm 37:23; 119:105; Proverbs 19:20; 27:17; Matthew 28:18–20; Acts 16:6–8; Romans 1:9–11; 12:4–8; 1 Corinthians 12:4–27; Ephesians 4:4–16; Philippians 2:13; 4:6,7; 2 Timothy 3:16,17; James 1:5; 1 John 5:14,15

Outline

   I. Select one decision
  II. Evaluate your talents
 III. Six ways God communicates with us
     A. In prayer
     B. Through the Bible
     C. By the Holy Spirit

D. Through Spirit-filled Christians
E. In providential circumstances
F. Through our desires

IV. The heart of the Sound Mind Principle
A. Ask God to reveal His will.
B. Determine the options in your decision.
C. Consult God's Word for principles.
D. Collect all pertinent information, and consider godly counsel.
E. Look at providential circumstances.
F. Examine your desires under the lordship of Jesus Christ.
G. "Listen" to the Holy Spirit.

V. Fill out a Pro/Con Chart

Leader's Preparation

The Christian life might be compared to a soldier in battle. He is out on the front lines, but is connected with his commanding officer by radio. We can use this metaphor to describe how God directs our lives.

First, during training a soldier thoroughly studies his training manual. Much of it he knows by heart, and if he has a question about procedure, he consults his manual promptly.

I am sure you recognize the similarity to a Christian's dependence on God's holy Word. It is our training manual, our guidebook for every part of our lives. Through His Word, God communicates His desires for us and His plan for our lives. Our responsibility is to study our guidebook daily, be familiar with its principles, and memorize its commands.

Second, a good soldier calls and tells his commanding officer of the conditions he faces. The soldier realizes that he could never adequately plot battle strategy from the field because he does not have a clear view of the entire battleground. Then commanding officer, who has an overview of the battle area and strategies from his vantage point, relays instructions to the soldier.

Similarly, the Christian shares his joys and sorrows, his victories and defeats, and his needs with his commanding officer, our heavenly Father. The Christian also trusts God to guide him through prayer and the Bible.

Third, a good soldier does not fight alone. He works with a team committed to achieving the same goal as he is. He listens to their advice, especially if they are battle veterans. The soldier discusses with them how he can best carry out the commander's orders in his particular corner of the field, and he coordinates his activities with his teammates so together they can function effectively to complete the goal.

Can you see the parallel between teamwork on a battlefield and teamwork within the Body of Christ, the worldwide Church? None of us can effectively live godly lives and help win the world for Jesus Christ without the support of other Christians. When we face difficult decisions, their counsel is very valuable. In a similar way, communication with God and receiving the advice of godly counselors are essential to good decision-making. These three points are central to discovering God's will through the Sound Mind Principle. This lesson covers the basic steps of the Sound Mind Principle: asking God to reveal His will, determining your options, consulting God's Word, considering godly counsel, looking at providential circumstances, examining your desires, and "listening" to the Holy Spirit.

As you lead this session, look for ways to apply these steps to your life. Give examples of how you plan to use the Sound Mind Principle to make wise decisions, and gently guide your students to do the same in the decisions they must make. Ask questions such as: "What principles do you find in God's Word for this situation?" "What impressions has the Holy Spirit given you about the decision you must make?" "Have you received the counsel of other Christians?"

If a member desires, allow him to consult the group about any decision on which he wants to receive godly counsel. Also, be ready to suggest a pastor, counselor, or other godly Christians to whom you can refer your students.

Bring your flip chart and several Bible concordances to this session.

The Bible Study Session

Sharing (5 minutes)

Talk about the experiences you and your students have had walking in the Spirit since the last session. Discuss how walking in the Spirit helps you focus on making good decisions. Encourage students to contrast the differences between decisions made in the power of the Holy Spirit and decisions made under our own power.

Discussion Starter (5 minutes)

Say: Let me give you an example of a difficult decision one Christian made. **Read:**

> Campus Crusade for Christ offers summer projects to help college students learn how to share their faith and make disciples of new believers. The projects also help the students influence their communities for Christ through full-time jobs.
>
> Dave, a new Christian at the Hampton Beach Summer Project in New Hampshire, was involved in sharing his faith in the evenings. During the day, he worked at a convenience store. One week after beginning his job, he ran into a serious problem. The store carried a supply of pornographic magazines that clerks were expected to sell to customers who requested them. As a believer, Dan felt he could not sell these materials.
>
> Dan went to Jim, the summer project director, and explained that he could not offer people new life in Christ by night and sell them destruction by day. Instead of giving Dan a pat answer to his problem, Jim challenged Dan to find God's solution.

Ask:

- If you were Dan, how would you find God's solution to this problem?

- What do you know for sure about God's will in Dan's situation?

- What are some of the options Dan has?
- What is the likely result of choosing each of these options?

Say: Here is what happened to Dan. **Read:**

Dan knew that God warns us against dwelling on lust (Colossians 3:5). He asked the convenience store owner to discontinue selling the magazines. The employer's attitude was that since someone was going to make money selling the magazines, it might as well be him.

So Dan proposed a deal. He promised to pray that God would compensate the owner for any lost profit from the magazine sales if he would remove the magazines. The owner was so shocked by Dan's convictions and so impressed by his faith that he removed the magazines.[5]

Ask:

- If Dan had lost his job over this decision, what would that say about his choice?
- How would you have handled this same situation?

Lesson Development (20 minutes)

Select One Decision

Say: For this session, I want you to think of a decision you must make this week to which you can apply the steps we will be learning. The decision does not have to be a major one, but a choice that is difficult enough that you do not have a ready answer about the direction you will take. Write that decision in your Study Guide. **Give students a few moments to think of a decision and write it in their books.**

Then say: Before we begin discussing these steps, let us review what we covered during our last session. First, let me read the definition of the Sound Mind Principle:

The Sound Mind Principle of 2 Timothy 1:7 means a well-balanced mind that is under the control of the Holy Spirit, transformed according to Romans 12:1,2.

---

[5] Adapted from *Worldwide Challenge*, March/April 1996.

Ask:

- To have the mind of Christ, which three questions do we ask ourselves?

    1. *(Why did Jesus come to Earth? Luke 19:10—To seek and save the lost.)*

    2. *(What is the greatest experience of your life?—To know Christ personally as my Savior and Lord.)*

    3. *(Then what is the greatest thing you can do to help others? —Introduce them to Christ.)*

Say: Therefore, our priority in life is to help fulfill Christ's mission to seek and save the lost. That is called helping to fulfill the Great Commission. Let us turn in our Bibles to where Jesus gave the Great Commission, Matthew 28:18–20. **Read Matthew 28:18–20.** We also learned that faith is the key to helping fulfill the Great Commission and to discovering God's will. **Ask:**

- What three factors must exist before you can discern God's will?

    1. *(There is no unconfessed sin in my life.)*

    2. *(I am fully dedicated to God and am filled with the Holy Spirit.)*

    3. *(I am walking in the Spirit moment by moment.)*

Say: Right now, let us take a few moments to make sure these factors exist in our lives. Silently reflect on and pray about these three factors. If God reveals sin in your life, confess it. Then ask the Holy Spirit to fill you with His power. **Give students a few moments to pray. Then say:** Now that we have prepared our hearts to do God's will, the next step is to evaluate our talents in light of our priority to seek and save the lost. This will help give us more understanding on ways we can help fulfill Christ's mission.

Evaluate Your Talents

Say: Every sincere Christian will want to make his God-given time, talents, and treasure available to Christ so that his fullest potential will be realized for our Lord. For one Christian, this talent may be preaching, evangelism, or teaching. For another, it may be business skills. For still another, it may be administration or service to others. For others, it may be staying at home to care for young children.

God has given each of us unique talents and abilities. He has also provided training for each person in His family through the local church, secular or religious education, the school of experience, and other sources. Let us read several passages of Scripture and identify the most important ideas about how we should use our talents for the good of the Body of Christ.

Form three groups and assign each group one of the following passages. Give them a few minutes to read the verses and discuss the question, then ask each group to report on the answers they gave. Encourage students to take notes in their Study Guides. To guide the discussion, suggested answers are given for you.

- According to these verses, how should our talents and abilities be used to further God's kingdom?

  Romans 12:4–8 *(Recognize that my gifts are different than those of others; I should use my gift according to its purpose for helping the Church; I should have a right attitude in using my gifts.)*

  1 Corinthians 12:4–27 *(Although there are many gifts, I need to recognize that the Spirit gives them all; my gift is to be used for the common good; the Spirit gives gifts as He wills; there are no lesser gifts, the Body of Christ needs every believer's talents; I should consider every believer's gifts valuable so that I do not cause division in the Church.)*

  Ephesians 4:4–16 *(Although there are many gifts in the Church, there is only one God who gives them to us; our gifts are to be used to equip believers for service and to build up the Church; God gives us gifts to help us mature in our faith.)*

When the discussion is finished, say: Now turn in your Study Guides to the section "Evaluate Your Talents." Jot down some of the talents and abilities God has given you. Remember, no talent is insignificant to God. Then list the training your have received and a few of your most dominant personality traits and other qualities. Part of your training may be attendance in Sunday school classes, a good friend's spiritual guidance in your life, opportunities you have had in ministry, or classes you have taken.

Give students a few minutes to reflect and write. Then say: We learn how to use our talents through communicating with God. If I asked you to name ways God communicates with us, you probably could give me several answers. Let us look at six ways God helps us find His will.

Six Ways God Communicates With Us

Say: When our hearts are open to doing God's will, He shows us what He wants us to do. He communicates with us in six ways. **Write each point on your flip chart and read the verses. Give students time to write the point in their Study Guides and record examples of times when God communicated to them in this way.**

1. *In prayer* (Philippians 4:6,7; James 1:5–7). Seeking God's wisdom will bring us peace.

2. *Through the Bible* (Psalm 119:105; 2 Timothy 3:16,17). The most important step in finding God's will is to seek His will as revealed in Scripture.

3. *By the Holy Spirit* (John 14:26; Acts 16:6–8). Submitting to the Holy Spirit's leading will give us power and direction in our lives.

4. *Through Spirit-filled Christians* (Proverbs 15:22; 19:20). Weighing their counsel will help us see aspects of the situation we have missed.

5. *In providential circumstances* (Genesis 50:18–20). Like Joseph, we can see God at work in our circumstances, which will help us know God's will.

6. *Through our desires* (Romans 1:9–11). As we submit our wants to the lordship of Jesus Christ, He gives us the desires of our hearts.

Application (20–30 minutes)

The Heart of the Sound Mind Principle

Say: Now let us look at each of these areas in greater depth as we go on to the heart of the Sound Mind Principle. Remember: When we apply the Sound Mind Principle, we do not use it as a formula that can solve all of our problems in decision-making, but as a plan to help us find God's will for our lives. Plans are flexible; formulas are rigid. With this in mind, let us apply these six areas of communication to the decisions we jotted down in our Study Guides.

1. Ask God to reveal His will.

Say: Our first step is to ask God to show us what He wants us to do. To do so, we can claim this promise, "The steps of a good man are directed by the Lord (Psalm 37:23, TLB). We also have this biblical assurance, which we studied earlier: **Read 1 John 5:14,15.** Right now, ask God to reveal His will concerning the decision you wrote in your Study Guide by claiming the promise in James 1:5-7. He will give you wisdom when you ask in faith. **Give students a few moments to pray silently.**

2. Determine the options in your decision.

Say: Making good choices means evaluating your options. In your Study Guide, write down the options of your decision in the space provided. List all areas, even if some seem unlikely. This is an important part of the decision-making process, so take your time to think through all aspects of your decision. **Give students a few moments to write down their options.**

3. Consult God's Word for principles you can apply to your decision.

Say: There are some things we can know for sure about God's will. For instance, the Bible tells us not to lie or steal. If one of your options would clearly violate a scriptural command or principle, you will know immediately that this choice is not God's will. Robert, for example, was offered a lucrative sales job, but it required him to employ questionable tactics to manipulate customers into buying a product. Since the Bible gives numerous warnings against dishonesty, his decision to turn down the job offer was the right choice.

We know God would never lead us to options that would require us to break His moral laws. As we spend time in God's Word each day, memorize verses, and study its wisdom, we will find these unchangeable principles. God has promised that His Word will guide us. **Read 2 Timothy 3:16,17.**

We can also search His Word for answers to our questions about all of our options. Whenever you are seeking God's will in a decision, use a Bible concordance to steer you to appropriate verses. Select key words that describe your options and look them up in the concordance. For example, if you are planning to borrow money to buy a car, look up words such as money, borrow, or spend. You may want to read the appropriate verses in several translations of the Bible.

As you study God's Word, ask yourself these three questions:

- Who is speaking in this passage?

- Who is God addressing? The nation of Israel, unbelievers, the worldwide Church, people in general, or an individual?

- How can this verse apply to my life, not just as information, but as God speaking to me personally to help me know His will?

If you brought Bible concordances with you, make them available to the group members or encourage members to use the concordance in the back of their Bibles.

Give students a few minutes to look up verses that may apply to their decisions.

4. Collect all pertinent information, and consider godly counsel.

Say: Making decisions without adequate information can lead to tragedy. Gathering all necessary information in decision-making is like having a road map on a trip through rugged mountains. You cannot see ahead very far because of the twists and turns in the road. Dense forest blocks your view. But a map gives you insight into where the road will take you. In a similar way, appropriate information can help give a sense of direction or map out road blocks you may not realize are in your way.

Receiving godly counsel is another important element in decision-making. As we read in the verses about the Body of Christ, we are part of an active, worldwide Church and we should be part of a local church, too. God wants us to support each other and to care for each other. That is one reason we are meeting together in this Bible study rather than covering the material on our own.

For each major decision you make, ask Spirit-filled Christians who know the Word of God for their views on your options. Then prayerfully consider their counsel. However, do not make the counsel of others a crutch. Although God often speaks to us through the advice of other Christians, He instructs us to place our trust solely in Him.

In your Study Guide, write the names of several Christians whom you could consult for godly counsel. **Give students a few moments to write.**

5. Look at providential circumstances.

In Step 2, we discussed the dangers of relying solely on the closed- or open-door policy for determining God's will. But God often uses circumstances to direct us. To determine whether your options are a part of God's will or a barrier He is using to direct you somewhere else, take into account these four basic factors: the authority of Scripture, providential circumstances, conviction based on reason, and impressions of the Holy Spirit. If providential circumstances coincide with the other three factors, then you can be assured that God is leading through your circumstances. If you find that the four factors do not agree, however, trust God to move the mountain of circumstances based on what you believe He has led you to do or pursue another option as God leads you. **Ask:**

- How have you seen God use circumstances to guide you in a particular direction? *(Allow volunteers to respond.)*

- How have you seen God work in the middle of circumstances that seemed like a mountain blocking you from doing God's will? *(Allow volunteers to respond.)*

- How did you know the difference between the two? *(Discuss as a group.)*

6. Examine your desires under the lordship of Jesus Christ.

Say: Our heartfelt desires are not automatically wrong. In fact, when we walk daily in the Spirit and sincerely commit ourselves to doing God's will, our desires can be a valid part of His leading. But our desires cannot be the sole or most important means for making decisions. They must always be submitted to the lordship of Jesus Christ. **Ask:**

- Think of a time when God met the desires of your heart. What happened? *(Allow for responses.)*

- Now think of a time when God changed your desires. How did that occur? *(Allow for responses.)*

7. "Listen" to the Holy Spirit.

Say: Many mature Christians will tell you how God has led them in certain directions by impressions of the Holy Spirit on their minds. "Listening" to the Holy Spirit in this way can be a valid means of knowing God's will, but only when we can say yes to these four questions:

- Will the impression you have give honor and glory to God?

- Is it consistent with God's Word?

- Will it bring blessing to the body of Christ?

- Has it received the blessing of godly Christians?

Say: Right now, meditate on your decision in light of the principles you discovered in God's Word. Do not feel that you must receive an "impression," but be open to the Holy Spirit's guidance. Although we will take a few moments to pray right now, this step may be more appropriate when you are alone with God and have more time to seek His heart for your decision. **Give students a few moments to meditate and pray.**

Say: Now look at your options once more. Is God's will becoming clearer? Do you have an idea of what you should do? Let us put what we learned about our options into a Pro/Con Chart. An example is given for you. First, let us read through the sample chart to get an idea of how to fill one out. **Read through the sample chart to make sure everyone understands how to complete it.**

Continue: Now write your decision and options in the blank chart. Then list the pros and cons for each option. When you finish, ask yourself, "Where or how, according to the Sound Mind Principle, can the Lord Jesus Christ, through my yielded life, accomplish the most in continuing His great ministry of seeking and saving the lost?" As you work through this process, you will find that this procedure will result in positive actions leading to God's perfect will for your life. Take a few moments to begin filling out the chart for the decision you jotted down earlier.

Give students time to work part-way through the chart. Then encourage them to complete the chart on their own before the next session.

Pro/Con Chart

Decision: What should I do after I graduate from college?							
Enter Politics		Get a Master's Degree		Find a Job as an Engineer		Join Staff of a Christian Ministry	
Pro	Con	Pro	Con	Pro	Con	Pro	Con
Greater influence on community	Stressful position	Higher salary	More school	High salary	Less time for ministry, fellowship	Serving the Lord full-time	Limited salary
Able to bring godly principles to legislation	Little job security	Greater credibility with future employers	Parents not too positive	Fulfills my dream	May require a move	Receiving training, spiritual growth	Non-Christian parents not supportive
Position will open doors for the gospel	Limited time to serve God, have family	Recommended by career counselor	Will not be able to help my brother through school	Presents opportunities for sharing gospel	Less time for discipling others	Best opportunity for sharing the gospel	

Pro/Con Chart

Decision:							
Options:							
Pro	**Con**	**Pro**	**Con**	**Pro**	**Con**	**Pro**	**Con**

1. Write down the decision you must make.

2. List each option along with all pros and cons.

3. To evaluate each option, ask the two questions below:

   ■ For each item in the Pro column, ask, "Will this help to fulfill the Great Commission?

   ■ After you review each column, ask, "Which of these options do I believe will maximize my impact in helping to fulfill the Great Commission?"

Say: In our next session, we will look at two final aspects of the Sound Mind Principle. Then we will put all this together into a few steps that you can apply to any situation. Once you have used the process a few times, it will become easy to apply.

Remember to complete your Pro/Con Chart before our next session together.

Closing and Prayer (5 minutes)

Close by asking volunteers to pray sentence prayers. Encourage group members to pray for the decision they examined in this session.

If you are planning another Bible study after this one ends, talk to your group about different topics. The resources listed at the back of the Study Guide give suggestions for other Bible studies you can lead.

Follow-Up

Since this is your next-to-last session, plan another get-together for fellowship. Now that your group members have gotten to know each other, hold an informal gathering in someone's home or other place in which everyone can relate comfortably. If appropriate, invite group members' spouses who do not attend and their children so the group can get to know each other's families.

Student Lesson Plan

Select One Decision

One decision I must make this week is:

Evaluate Your Talents

Every sincere Christian will want to make his God-given time, talents, and treasure available to Christ so that his fullest potential will be realized for our Lord. Read these passages of Scripture and identify the most important ideas about how we should use our talents for the good of the Body of Christ.

Romans 12:4–18

1 Corinthians 12:4–27

Ephesians 4:4–16

My God-given talents and abilities are:

The training I have received is:

My personality traits and other qualities are:

Six Ways God Communicates With Us

When our hearts are open to doing God's will, He shows us what He wants us to do. He communicates with us in six ways. Write each point and record an example of a time when God communicated to you in this way.

1.

Example:

2.

Example:

3.

Example:

4.

Example:

5.

Example:

6.

Example:

The Heart of the Sound Mind Principle

Write down each step of the Sound Mind Principle. Apply the related questions to the decision you are considering.

1.

2.

My options are:

3.

As you study God's Word, ask yourself these three questions:

- Who is speaking in this passage?

- Who is God addressing? The nation of Israel, unbelievers, the worldwide Church, people in general, or an individual?

- How can this verse apply to my life, not just as information, but as God speaking to me personally to help me know His will?

4.

Pertinent information about my decision is:

Several Christians I can consult for godly counsel are:

5.

- How have you seen God use circumstances to guide you in a particular direction?

- How have you seen God work in the middle of circumstances that seemed like a mountain blocking you from doing God's will?

- How did you know the difference between the two?

6.

- Think of a time when God met the desires of your heart. What happened?

- Now think of a time when God changed your desires. How did that occur?

7.

"Listening" to the Holy Spirit can be a valid means of knowing God's will, but only when we can say yes to these four questions:

- Will the impression you have give honor and glory to God?

- Is it consistent with God's Word?

- Will it bring blessing to the body of Christ?

- Has it received the blessing of godly Christians?

Review this chart for an example of how to fill one out.

Pro/Con Chart

Decision: What should I do after I graduate from college?							
Enter Politics		Get a Master's Degree		Find a Job as an Engineer		Join Staff of a Christian Ministry	
Pro	Con	Pro	Con	Pro	Con	Pro	Con
Greater influence on community	Stressful position	Higher salary	More school	High salary	Less time for ministry, fellowship	Serving the Lord full-time	Limited salary
Able to bring godly principles to legislation	Little job security	Greater credibility with future employers	Parents not too positive	Fulfills my dream	May require a move	Receiving training, spiritual growth	Non-Christian parents not supportive
Position will open doors for the gospel	Limited time to serve God, have family	Recommended by career counselor	Will not be able to help my brother through school	Presents opportunities for sharing gospel	Less time for discipling others	Best opportunity for sharing the gospel	

Pro/Con Chart

Decision:							
Options:							
Pro	Con	Pro	Con	Pro	Con	Pro	Con

1. Write down the decision you must make.

2. List each option along with all pros and cons.

3. To evaluate each option, ask the two questions below:

- For each item in the Pro column, ask, "Will this help to fulfill the Great Commission?

- After you review each column, ask, "Which of these options do I believe will maximize my impact in helping to fulfill the Great Commission?"

S T E P 5

By Faith, Follow God's Leading

Focus

The final steps in discerning God's will are to follow God's commands by faith and confirm circumstances surrounding the decision.

Objectives

This session will help students to:

- *Discuss* how Christ submitted to God's will

- *Learn* how to follow God's command by faith

- *Confirm* the decision through circumstances

- *Apply* the Sound Mind Principle as a whole

Session Scriptures

Psalm 40:8; Matthew 6:10; Mark 3:31–34; Luke 22:39–44; John 4:34; Acts 4:32—5:11; 21:12–14; 1 Corinthians 4:1,2; Philippians 2:12,13; 4:19; Hebrews 10:5–7; 11:6; James 4:13–15

Outline

    I. Jesus Christ is our supreme example
   II. By faith, follow God's commands
  III. Confirming your decision
  IV. Steps to making a sound mind decision

Leader's Preparation

To prepare for this session, meditate on the following passages of Scripture during your quiet times. As you study these verses, reflect on how each person followed God's will regardless of their circumstances.

- Esther approached the king to plead for the lives of her people even though that meant risking her own life (Esther 4:1—5:2).

- Daniel prayed to God even though he knew the king had decreed death for his actions (Daniel 6:1–11).

- Stephen was martyred for his faith (Acts 6:8–15; 7:54–60).

- Paul was stoned, beaten, and imprisoned for preaching the gospel (Acts 14:19–21; 16:22–25; 21:27–36).

Since this lesson presents the entire scope of the Sound Mind Principle, be sure to give your group enough time to complete the Application section of this lesson. This should take about twenty minutes. If you need more time or if your students have quite a few questions about the Sound Mind decision-making process, plan to meet individually with those students.

Also, review Steps 3 and 4 to help you understand the broad scope of the Sound Mind Principle. You might also review with the group any areas of Steps 1 through 4 that your students have expressed difficulty understanding or applying.

Remember, leading a Bible study is more than a five-week responsibility. After your study ends, keep in contact with your students and encourage them in their decision-making. Remind them that new concepts, such as the Sound Mind Principle, take time to integrate into their lives. Each time your students use the principle, they will become more familiar with it and will use it more frequently.

The Bible Study Session

Sharing (5 minutes)

Ask volunteers to share what happened with the decisions they considered during the last session. Encourage students who are still working through their situations to

be patient and wait for the Lord's timing and guidance. Point out how God worked differently in each decision.

Discussion Starter (5 minutes)

Say: Henry Blackaby and Claude King write in their book *Experiencing God*:

> When God asks you to do something that you cannot do, you will face a crisis of belief. You will have to decide what you really believe about God. Can He and will He do what He has said He wants to do through you? What you do in response to His invitation reveals what you believe about God regardless of what you say.[6]

Ask:

- Think of a time when you felt God was leading you to do something that was beyond your ability to accomplish. What was it?

- Did this situation cause you to doubt your ability to accomplish your task? Explain.

- How did your response show what you believed about God at that time?

- How did facing the decision cause you to change your ideas about God?

Lesson Development (30 minutes)

Jesus Christ Is Our Supreme Example

Say: To begin our session today, let us look at the supreme example of a person who followed God's will to the letter. That person, of course, is our Lord and Savior, Jesus Christ.

Form two groups. Instruct each group to read Luke 22:39–44 and discuss these questions:

- What attitude did Jesus have?

---

[6] Henry T. Blackaby and Claude V. King, *Experiencing God*, Nashville, TN: Broadman & Holman Publishers, 1994, p. 36.

- What conclusion did Jesus reach about the decision He had to make?

- What can we learn from His example that will help us in making decisions?

Give groups time to discuss the questions and write answers in their Study Guides, then have each group report their answers. After your discussion, direct students to the passages under the questions. Ask:

- What else can we learn about Christ's attitude from these verses?

  John 4:34 *(His greatest desire was to do God's will.)*

  Hebrews 10:5–7 *(He was submissive to God's will because He was prepared beforehand for this purpose.)*

Then say: As with most things, attitude makes the difference. When we have a servant attitude, we will discover and follow God's will. **Ask:**

- What one word could you use to describe the believer's attitude in the following passages?

As a group, read each passage and brainstorm words to describe each attitude. Some suggestions are given for you.

- Psalm 40:8 *(Delight; desire.)*
- Matthew 6:10 *(Submissiveness.)*
- Acts 21:12–14 *(Faithfulness; acceptance.)*
- Philippians 2:12,13 *(Yieldedness; obedience.)*
- James 4:13–15 *(Humility.)*

Say: Jesus also described how important He considered doing God's will. These verses show us His attributes. **Read Mark 3:31–34. Ask:**

- How would you describe Jesus' statement in your own words? *(Allow volunteers to respond.)*

Say: Obeying God's will is essential for two reasons. First, we prosper as Christians and grow spiritually as we follow His commands. Second, we accomplish God's purpose for our life and ministry.

To put these reasons into perspective, let us review what we have learned. In our last Bible study session, we discussed several steps we can follow in discerning God's will. They are:

1. Ask God to reveal His will to you.
2. Determine your options.
3. Consult God's Word.
4. Consider godly counsel.
5. Look at providential circumstances.
6. Examine your desires under the lordship of Jesus Christ.
7. "Listen" to the Holy Spirit.

Each of us applied these seven steps to one decision. These steps lead us to the last step in our pathway to finding God's will—by faith, follow God's commands.

By Faith, Follow God's Commands

Think of following God's commands by faith like this: Just as turning the steering wheel of an automobile does not alter its direction unless it is moving, God cannot direct our lives unless we are moving for Him. But when to take action may not always be clear. **Ask:**

- What is the difference between waiting on the Lord to reveal His will and not moving in the direction God leads? *(In the first, a person is actively seeking God's will; in the second, a person is ignoring God's will.)*

- What part does faith play in moving out for God? *(By faith, we step out and do what God asks us to do; our faith enables us get started in the right direction.)*

Say: Just as you received Christ as your Savior by faith, you also live your Christian walk by faith. In fact, faith is the essence of our relationship with God. **Read Hebrews 11:6.** Everything we do reflects our faith or lack of faith.

Direct students to the two numbered points under "By Faith, Follow God's Commands" in their Study Guides. Then say: Once you come to an understanding of God's will in your area of need, by faith:

1. Be obedient to Him by following His commands and adhering to His guidelines as written in the Bible.

2. Trust the Holy Spirit to enable you to obey God so that the outcome of your decision and actions will be in accordance with His perfect will.

Confirming Your Decision

Say: When you have stepped out in faith to follow God's leading, confirmation that you are following God's will may come in various ways. Usually, the confirmation is a quiet, peaceful assurance that you are doing what God wants you to do. You will also have an expectancy that God will use you to bear fruit.

This confirmation can show you that you are on the right track. Having peace about a decision does not necessarily mean that the decision will lead to peaceful circumstances. Doing the right thing often means facing more turmoil than taking the easy way out. But the peace of mind and heart that God gives when we are in His will does not depend on circumstances. Do not mistake obstacles and difficulties or satanic opposition as a door closed by God. Many people in the Bible were sure that they were in God's will, yet they experienced difficult trials. **Ask:**

- Which believer in the Old or New Testament stands out as an example of a person who experienced difficulties while doing God's will? *(Examples: Esther approached the king to plead for the lives of her people even though that meant risking her own life; Daniel prayed to God even when the king decreed death for his actions; Stephen was martyred for his faith; Paul was stoned, beaten, and imprisoned for his faith.)*

- What quality did that person display that helped him or her continue following God's will? *(Allow volunteers to respond.)*

Say: Christians who follow the guidance of the Holy Spirit will often encounter spiritual opposition. When you do, keep your eyes on Jesus. He is your life, your peace, your victory, your wisdom, and your strength. As we read in Psalm 40:8, delight yourself in doing His will.

As you seek God's will, be alert to two common self-deceptions, which are given in your Study Guide.

1. Do not try to manipulate God into doing your will by bargaining with Him or trying to deceive Him. In other words, do not make plans in your fleshly nature and expect God to bless them.

Ask several students to read Acts 4:32—5:11 and answer these questions in the Study Guide:

- Why did Ananias and Sapphira try to deceive the apostles? *(They wanted to keep part of the money for themselves yet appear to have given it all so they would seem righteous.)*

- Why do you think God used an immediate punishment? *(He wanted to show the new Church that He sees all of our motives and actions.)*

Say: Ananias and Sapphira did not act wrongly by keeping a portion of their money. They sinned when they claimed that they had given it all, showing that they had a higher regard for what men think of them than what God thinks. Their problem was not lack of generosity, but dishonesty and lack of concern for God's will.

2. Do not deceive yourself by trying to justify your wants as God's will. Distinguish between needs and greeds. God promises to meet your needs.

Read Philippians 4:19. Then ask students to read 1 Corinthians 4:1,2 and answer the questions in their Study Guides as you discuss them as a group.

- How does considering yourself a steward of what God has given you help you separate need from greed? *(If I consid-*

*er myself as a manager rather than an owner of my posses-
sions, I won't want to hang onto them or to accumulate
wealth for selfish reasons.)*

■ How does the principle of stewardship help us keep our
time and talents in line with God's will? *(We understand
that our time and talents belong to God; we will use them for
His purposes rather than for our own selfish desires.)*

Say: As we learn more about the Lord and His commands
and learn to rely continually on the leading and empowering of
the Holy Spirit, we discover that our wills are conforming more
and more to God's will as it says in Romans 12:1,2.

Our goal, therefore, is to mature toward knowing the mind
of Christ. Then when we make decisions, we will make them in
the knowledge of what Christ wants for us. When action is
taken, we move in the direction that Christ would go and do the
things that He would do.

God's way is always best and is the way of joy, excitement,
and adventure. Even during times of difficulty, each day can be
filled with blessing from God as we continue to walk in faith and
obedience.

As the last activity in our study, let us look at the Sound
Mind Principle as a complete process.

Application (15–20 minutes)

Steps to Making a Sound Mind Decision

**Some of the steps given in this section were covered in
the Application section of the previous lesson. The focus
of this lesson is to give the complete process for applying
the Sound Mind Principle. Going through the steps once
more will give students a firmer grasp of how to use the
principle in their own lives.**

Say: The following instructions are the ten steps of the
Sound Mind Principle. Take the next few minutes to use this
principle to examine one of your life goals, such as the direction

of your career or personal ministry over the next ten years. I will give you ten to fifteen minutes to work through the steps. If you like, you may work with a partner and discuss how to make your decisions.

Give students ten to fifteen minutes to work through the steps. Then discuss any questions they may have.

Use these steps to help you make your decision.

1. Ask God to reveal His will.

   - Be sure Christ is Lord of your life and that you are walking in the fullness and power of the Holy Spirit (Ephesians 5:18).

   - Be sure there is no unconfessed sin in your life (Psalm 66:18).

   - Pray for wisdom (James 1:5,6).

2. Determine the options in your decision.

3. Search the Bible for any relevant principles and commands.

   To do so, review these key questions:

   - Why did Jesus come (Luke 19:10)?—To seek and save the lost.

   - What is the most important experience in your life?—Receiving Christ.

   - What is the most important thing you can do for others?—Help them come to know Christ as Savior.

   - Considering the answers to these questions, which option in this decision will best maximize your ability to help fulfill the Great Commission?

4. Collect all available information and the counsel of mature believers on each option.

5. Look at providential circumstances.

6. Examine your desires under the lordship of Jesus Christ.

7. Listen to the Holy Spirit.

8. List all options with their advantages and disadvantages on the Pro/Con chart.

9. Trust God for His wisdom, evaluate the options, and make a decision according to His promises in Psalm 37:23 and Proverbs 3:5,6.

10. Take steps to act on your decision by faith. Do not depend on feelings. God promises real wisdom and the inner peace that only He can give, not just a fleeting feeling about the decision you made.

Action Point: Prayerfully consider the following decision:

After applying the Sound Mind Principle of Scripture to determine God's will for my future, I feel God is leading me to invest my life to help fulfill the Great Commission in the following ways:

_____

_____

_____

_____ *(Signature)*

Closing and Prayer

When students finish, say: As you sincerely and diligently study the Scriptures and allow our all-wise, sovereign heavenly Father to control your life, you will experience the most joyful, abundant, and fruitful life of all. Expect the Lord Jesus Christ to draw men to Himself through you. As you begin each day, acknowledge the fact that you belong to Him. Thank Him for living within you, and invite Him to use your mind to think His thoughts, your heart to express His love, your lips to speak His truth. Ask our Lord Jesus Christ to be at home in your life and to walk around in your body that He may continue to seek and save souls through you. This kind of life is our rightful heritage in Christ, and we can fully appropriate all that God has given us by using the Sound Mind Principle as a way of life.

Lead your group in closing prayer of thankfulness to God and ask Him to guide each of you in the decisions you face.

Follow-Up

If you have decided to continue your group study with another topic, set the time and date for your next meeting. If you are discontinuing your group study, invite members to keep in contact and to support each other in making godly decisions.

Encourage each of your students to start the *Five Steps to Knowing God's Will* Bible study with their own group. Help interested students to select group members through personal contacts, advertising in the campus paper or a senior citizen magazine, or other appropriate means. (Refer to the section "How to Lead a Small-Group Bible Study" in the introduction of this book.) Attend your students' first Bible study meeting if possible to help them get started.

Student Lesson Plan

Jesus Christ Is Our Supreme Example

Read Luke 22:39–44 and discuss these three questions:

- What attitude did Jesus have?

- What conclusion did Jesus reach about the decision He had to make?

- What can we learn from His example that will help us in making decisions?

What else can we learn about Christ's attitude from these verses?

John 4:34

Hebrews 10:5–7

As with most things, attitude makes the difference. When we have a servant attitude, we will discover and follow God's will. What one word could you use to describe the believer's attitude in the following passages?

Psalm 40:8

Matthew 6:10

Acts 21:12–14

Philippians 2:12,13

James 4:13–15

- Read Mark 3:31–34. How would you describe Jesus' statement in your own words?

Obeying God's will is essential for two reasons:

1. We prosper as Christians and grow spiritually as we follow His commands.

2. We accomplish God's purpose for our life and ministry.

By Faith, Follow God's Commands

Just as turning the steering wheel of an automobile does not alter its direction unless it is moving, God cannot direct our lives unless we are moving for Him.

- What is the difference between waiting on the Lord to reveal His will and not moving in the direction God leads?

- What part does faith play in moving out for God?

Once you come to an understanding of God's will in your area of need, by faith:

1. Be obedient to Him by following His commands and adhering to His guidelines as written in the Bible.

2. Trust the Holy Spirit to enable you to obey God so that the outcome of your decision and actions will be in accordance with His perfect will.

Confirming Your Decision

When you have stepped out in faith to follow God's leading, confirmation that you are following God's will may come in various ways. Usually, the confirmation is a quiet, peaceful assurance that you are doing what God wants you to do. You will also have an expectancy that God will use you to bear fruit.

- Which believer in the Old or New Testament stands out as an example of a person who experienced difficulties while doing God's will?

- What quality did that person display that helped him or her continue following God's will?

As you seek God's will for your situation, be alert to two common self-deceptions.

1. Do not try to manipulate God into doing your will by bargaining with Him or trying to deceive Him.

   Read Acts 4:32—5:11.

   - Why did Ananias and Sapphira try to deceive the apostles?

- Why do you think God used an immediate punishment?

2. Do not deceive yourself by trying to justify your wants as God's will. Distinguish between needs and greeds. God promises to meet your needs (Philippians 4:19).

   Read 1 Corinthians 4:1,2.

   - How does considering yourself a steward of what God has given you help you separate need from greed?

   - How does the principle of stewardship help us keep our time and talents in line with God's will?

Steps to Making a Sound Mind Decision

The following instructions are the ten steps of the Sound Mind Principle. Refer to these steps in the future for all the decisions you must make. Right now, use these steps to help you examine one of your life goals.

1. Ask God to reveal His will.

   - Be sure Christ is Lord of your life and that you are walking in the fullness and power of the Holy Spirit (Ephesians 5:18).

   - Be sure there is no unconfessed sin in your life (Psalm 66:18).

   - Pray for wisdom (James 1:5,6).

2. Determine the options in your decision.

3. Search the Bible for relevant principles and commands.

   To do so, review these key questions:

   - Why did Jesus come (Luke 19:10)?—To seek and save the lost.

   - What is the most important experience in your life?—Receiving Christ.

   - What is the most important thing you can do for others?—Help them come to know Christ as Savior.

- Considering the answers to these questions, which option in this decision will best maximize your ability to help fulfill the Great Commission?

4. Collect all available information and the counsel of mature believers on each option.

5. Look at providential circumstances.

6. Examine your desires under the lordship of Jesus Christ.

7. Listen to the Holy Spirit.

8. List all options with their advantages and disadvantages on the Pro/Con chart.

Pro/Con Chart

How to Maximize Your Life for the Glory of God
According to the Sound Mind Principle of Scripture

Decision:							
Options:							
Pro	Con	Pro	Con	Pro	Con	Pro	Con

1. Write down the decision you must make.

2. List each option along with all pros and cons.

3. To evaluate each option, ask the two questions below:

   - For each item in the Pro column, ask, "Will this help to fulfill the Great Commission?

   - After you review each column, ask, "Which of these options do I believe will maximize my impact in helping to fulfill the Great Commission?"

9. Trust God for His wisdom, evaluate the options, and make a decision according to His promises in Psalm 37:23 and Proverbs 3:5,6.

10. Take steps to act on your decision by faith. Do not depend on feelings. God promises real wisdom and the inner peace that only He can give, not just a fleeting feeling about the decision you made.

Action Point: Prayerfully consider the following decision.

After applying the Sound Mind Principle of Scripture to determine God's will for my future, I feel God is leading me to invest my life to help fulfill the Great Commission in the following ways:

_____

_____

_____

_____ *(Signature)*

 BILL BRIGHT is founder and president of Campus Crusade for Christ International. Serving in 155 major countries representing 98 percent of the world's population, he and his dedicated team of more than 113,000 full-time staff, associate staff, and trained volunteers have introduced tens of millions of people to Jesus Christ, discipling millions to live Spirit-filled, fruitful lives of purpose and power for the glory of God.

Dr. Bright did graduate study at Princeton and Fuller Theological seminaries from 1946 to 1951. The recipient of many national and international awards, including five honorary doctorates, he is the author of numerous books and publications committed to helping fulfill the Great Commission. His special focus is *NewLife2000*, an international effort to help reach more than six billion people with the gospel of our Lord Jesus Christ by the year 2000.

Response Form

☐ I have received Jesus Christ as my Savior and Lord as a result of reading this book.

☐ I am a new Christian and want to know Christ better and experience the abundant Christian life.

☐ I want to be one of the two million people who will join Dr. Bright in forty days of fasting and prayer for revival.

☐ Please send me **free** information on staff and ministry opportunities with Campus Crusade for Christ.

☐ Please send me **free** information about other books, booklets, audio cassettes, and videos by Bill Bright.

NAME_____

ADDRESS_____

CITY _____ STATE _____ ZIP _____

COUNTRY _____

Please check the appropriate box(es), clip, and mail this form in an envelope to:

Dr. Bill Bright
Campus Crusade for Christ
P.O. Box 593684
Orlando, FL 62859-3684

You may also fax your response to (407) 826-2149 or send E-mail to newlifepubs@ccci.org. Visit our Web site at www.newlifepubs.com.

This and other fine products from NewLife Publications are available from your favorite bookseller or by calling **(800) 235-7255, ext. 73** *(within U.S.) or* **(407) 826-2145, ext. 73** *(outside U.S.).*